The Human Side of Corporate Competitiveness

The Human Side of Corporate Competitiveness

Edited by
Daniel B. Fishman
Cary Cherniss

SAGE PUBLICATIONS
The International Professional Publishers
Newbury Park   London   New Delhi

For information address:

SAGE Publications, Inc.
2111 West Hillcrest Drive
Newbury Park, California 91320

SAGE Publications Ltd.
28 Banner Street
London EC1Y 8QE
England

SAGE Publications India Pvt. Ltd.
M-32 Market
Greater Kailash I
New Delhi 110 048 India

Printed in the United States of America

Library of Congress Cataloging-in-Publication Data

Main entry under title:

The Human side of corporate competitiveness / edited by Daniel B.
  Fishman, Cary Cherniss.
        p.   cm.
    Includes bibliographical references.
    ISBN 0-8039-3751-2. — ISBN 0-8039-3752-0 (pbk.)
    1. Industry—Social aspects. 2. Personnel management.
  3. Organizational change. 4. Work and family. I. Fishman, Daniel
  B.   II. Cherniss, Cary.
  HD60.H86   1990
  658—dc20   90-32538
                                                                  CIP

FIRST PRINTING, 1990

Sage Production Editor: Diane S. Foster

Contents

Preface

This book brings together the viewpoints of leading thinkers in the organizational field. It was stimulated through discussions between its two editors, who are members of the Organizational Behavior Program at the Graduate School of Applied and Professional Psychology (GSAPP) of Rutgers University, and leaders of the Corporate Human Resources Department at the Equitable Financial Companies. Orchestration of links among the various viewpoints and integration of themes among the different authors was facilitated by a two-day symposium held in October, 1988, and sponsored by Equitable and the Rutgers GSAPP. Each contributing author prepared a manuscript that was reviewed by the other authors before the symposium was held. The critical dialogue and interaction that was structured into the conference yielded substantial feedback to the authors, who then revised their manuscripts accordingly. This aspect of its origins, the extraordinary reputations and accomplishments of its authors, and the wide variety in types of experience, styles, and perspectives of these individuals have yielded what we believe to be an outstanding book.

Given the context of the book's development and the nature of its themes, it should be of particular interest to human resource departments in corporations, human resource managers in corporations, and business school faculty in departments of management, organizational behavior, human resources, and industrial relations. In addition, the book should be of great interest to those involved in applied psychology in specialty areas such as industrial, organizational, community, and human resources psychology. The book highlights the opportunities in professional psychology training and practice for emerging roles in dealing with the challenge of facilitating organizational competitiveness while promoting the health of workers, their families, and their communities. Since all of the authors are psychologists, they provide models of some of the roles in the human resources field in which the discipline of psychology can make a special contribution.

The symposium upon which this book is based was the fifth in a series of annual symposia on various topics in applied psychology. The Dean of the Rutgers Graduate School of Applied and Professional Psychology, Donald R. Peterson, initiated this symposium series and provided enormous support for this particular project. Without his enthusiastic leadership, neither the symposium nor this book would have been possible.

We also would like to acknowledge the very generous support of the Equitable Financial Companies, and particularly Joseph Radigan, Anita Underwood, and Charles Ballard, Jr., of Equitable's Corporate Human Resources Department. We originally had hoped to find a few corporate sponsors who could share the costs and risks involved in such an undertaking. We were immensely grateful when Equitable came forward and offered to underwrite the entire venture. However, their support went far beyond the financial. Joe Radigan graciously agreed to help open the symposium; his remarks from the perspective of a human resources executive, which subsequently were developed into a chapter for this book, provided an invaluable complement to the more academic views presented by others. Anita Underwood played a key role in developing the conceptual framework for the conference and devoted countless hours to the many details involved in its planning and execution. Chuck Ballard helped us to distill some of the central themes in his closing remarks and also helped Anita with some of the planning.

Equitable's financial support was augmented by a gift from Louella Buros, which made it possible for several faculty members and students from Rutgers University to attend the symposium free of charge.

Once planning for the symposium was underway, we received invaluable assistance from Diane Crino who coordinated the myriad of details involved in making sure that such an event went off smoothly. We also received much help from graduate students in the Organizational Behavior program at GSAPP, including Barbara Chas, John Pizutelli, Annette Riordan, Alyssa Chomiak, and Susanne Diggs.

Finally, we would like to acknowledge the contributors, who are not only outstanding leaders in the field, but also graciously adhered to our many deadlines and requests. Needless to say, we could not have produced this book without them. But more than that, they made this effort worthwhile and enjoyable as well.

—Daniel B. Fishman
—Cary Cherniss

PART I

Introduction

1 Setting the Scene: Can a Company Be Both Pro-Profits and Pro-People?

JOSEPH E. RADIGAN

This book explores the possibility of corporate strategies that allow companies to be both competitive in the marketplace and compassionate with their employees at the same time. Thus far, corporate emphasis has been largely on the competitive side. Indeed, over the last several years, we have witnessed an amazing quickening of the competitive spirit as companies strategically move into almost any niche that seems to offer profit and growth—niches that can capitalize on their unique people, technical resources, or reputation for quality and service.

As companies expanded beyond local markets into regions, and then went national and now global, their resources, corporate structure, business strategy, and human resource management capabilities were, and are, impacted by powerful forces—a changing socioeconomic environment, a new work force mix, organization changes, alterations in values, and the multicultural diversity of today's work force.

By the 1980s, business realized that traditional ways of doing business would no longer be enough because of the complex nature of worldwide competition. We had entered the era of cutthroat competition, mergers, acquisitions, corporate restructuring, and dreaded downsizing.

The United States, however, has always led the world in technological innovation, efficient manufacturing, and marketing expertise. Across the globe, U.S. service companies have demonstrated their competitive ability. In 1986, U.S. companies produced a record $48 billion of service exports. The true value of these exports may have been twice as much. Larger still are revenues of U.S. companies' overseas subsidiaries.

But new competitors are chipping away at the U.S. lead. In advertising, Saatchi and Saatchi of London are advertising's largest conglomerate; in banks and brokerage houses, Tokyo's giants dominate. The Japanese are also moving into construction, travel services, and hotels. In financial services, U.S. companies have no guaranteed advantage—despite the fact that the service sector will account for 80% of jobs in the U.S. by 1990. In fact, four of the world's five largest banks and four of its six largest securities houses are Japanese.

In the domestic financial field, we have the phenomenon of one-stop shopping, which has been spurred by deregulation. John Hancock maintains its right to do everything anybody else can do, and it has tried to enter the banking field with its "nonbank" bank. Metropolitan Life has entered the retail real estate field, while Prudential is heavily into capital markets. Sears, through Allstate, sells insurance right out of its stores. My own company, The Equitable Financial Companies, acquired 20 new businesses in the last few years. It has come a long way from being a conventional life insurance company.

As companies converge on the same fields, competition gets stiffer, and companies begin to find they are overdiversified and can't manage their key businesses. Primerica, for example, leveraged itself too much; it in turn has been taken over by Commercial Credit.

It takes huge amounts of capital investment to support a global business. And only the sturdy can survive when investors demand reasonable levels of return, particularly if expenses fund liberal benefits and supports for employees—the "compassion components" of the traditional employee relations program. There are also demands for better performance results. Thus, many companies have come to the overwhelming realization that they must cut costs in order to survive. Still fresh in the minds of corporate executives are the massive layoffs of 1987 in the wake of the cost-cutting imperative. Allegis, Firestone, General Motors, B. F. Goodrich, and Owens Illinois were among the companies that laid off very large numbers of employees, hoping to become more profitable. Unfortunately, this practice will continue. It is estimated that, with new technologies, everything produced now will, by 1995, be produced by 11 million fewer people. General Motors, for example, will be utilizing 22,000 robots. They will create 6,700 skilled jobs and eliminate production jobs. By 1995, more than half of all existing jobs will be changed and 30% will disappear (Johnston, 1987).

Another phenomenon affecting business survival and impacting people is the shift from labor-intensive to knowledge-intensive industries. About 70% of the cost of a semiconductor microchip, for example, consists of knowledge, while only about 12% is labor (Johnston, 1987). In the new information society, human capital is replacing dollar capital as the strategic, limiting resource that provides the competitive edge. In line with this, companies increasingly are starting to realize that they can earn more by being both pro-people *and* pro-profits than if they target profits as the only goal.

At the same time, other trends are transforming society: new competition for the best employees, the whittling away of middle management, the emergence of a new multicultural work force, and the revolution created by working mothers (Chira, 1989). For example, consider the following (Johnston, 1987):

> We are about to experience the oldest work force in recorded history. Career ladders are becoming crowded and opportunities for the "baby boom" generation of 25- to 44-year-olds are reduced.

> The "baby bust" generation of potential employees aged 16 to 24 is fewer in number and in great demand. The result is that, through 1995, significantly fewer workers will be available to fill entry-level jobs.

> Increasingly, the work force will be diverse. By 1990, 45% will be women; 15%, minorities; and 20%, guest laborers. In addition, 25% will live in single-parent households, and 55% will be white collar.

> It will be a seller's market for workers. Not only are fewer people entering the work force, but present trends indicate that there will be substantially more jobs to fill. During the 1970s, 20 million new jobs were created, but there was still unemployment; in the 1980s, selective labor shortages had started to occur. The shortage of unskilled labor is already critical.

> Corporations are going through an accelerated period of organizational change and restructuring. Between 1981 and 1983, half the Fortune 500 companies eliminated one layer of management, and it is estimated that 55% of all workers will require retraining to handle automation. Retraining experience, however, has not been encouraging because of workers' inability to adapt to high technology work and unwillingness to relocate or accept lower wages.

Still another important element in the overall picture is the stress among middle managers created by corporate restructurings and takeovers. These events are cutting out middle managers and increasing the workload of those who remain. It is harming them physically, emotionally, and mentally, and is frequently impairing performance, their families, and their lives. Company loyalty, which was always counted on, is rapidly disappearing.

The tangible costs of employee disability have hit employers hard. The major indicator, workers' compensation claims, reached $35 billion last year, double the 1980 level. Moreover, the definition of disability has been enlarged. These days, an emotional disorder originating far away from the job site will get a complainant just about as much compensation as a hernia or a bad back. While the rate of reported industrial accidents is actually falling, new categories of illness, including mental stress, are straining the workers' compensation system. In California alone, in 1986, injured workers and their employers ran up nearly one billion dollars in legal and medical bills. Claims for mental stress rose 531% between 1980 and 1986. In three out of four of the 7,000 cases the applicant cited job pressure. As another example, in Massachusetts, a recent court decision held that the emotional trauma from simply being fired may be compensable. While such claims are hard to prove, judges increasingly are sympathetic.

Until a few years ago, American middle managers had little reason to fear losing their jobs. Indeed, they were a protected class with virtual job security. When their companies suffered downturns, it was the blue-collar workers, not the managers, who lost their jobs. Not any more: cost-cutting American corporations have unilaterally cancelled the tacit contract of mutual fidelity they had with their managers. Fortune 500 companies alone eliminated almost 2.8 million jobs since 1980, 1 million of them managerial.

This may be a somewhat discouraging picture. Nevertheless, I believe that the experiences of the 1980s have provided an important learning experience that reinforces some of the old-fashioned truisms about people management.

Those of us who have not been mere armchair observers, but have been associated with major corporations that underwent restructuring and downsizing on a significant scale, can attest to the fact that without trust, respect, and mutual caring between management and its employees there can be pervasive cynicism, unpredictable outbursts of ill will, overt lack of cooperation, and destructive acts against the corporation. Employees want—yes, demand—decent treatment from employers, and when they don't perceive it is forthcoming, they vent their displeasure in unfortunate ways.

Is there a prescription, a solution perhaps? If change is in the air, and if downsize we must, are there ways to accomplish this and yet minimize the hurt and economic impact? These are the issues addressed in this book, and the various chapters offer informed, incisive analyses to better understand them and practical ideas for aiding us in accomplishing relevant goals. But in addition to ideas, we need courageous leadership committed to the belief that compassionate treatment of all employees is as important to the integrity and success of a corporation as quality performance and customer service.

References

Chira, S. (1989, October 1). In the 1990s, what price scarce labor? *New York Times*, pp. 29F, 33F.

Johnston, W. (1987). *Work force 2000*. Indianapolis, IN: Hudson Institute.

2 Overview: Development and Plan of the Book

DANIEL B. FISHMAN
CARY CHERNISS

How do we reconcile individual needs with organizational imperatives in the work place today? This question is not a new one. In fact, it is a modern version of one of the central problems in political philosophy, a problem that has been debated at least since the time of Plato.

But today this problem has become particularly urgent and timely as American industry attempts to regain its competitive advantage. There is probably a greater appreciation than ever before of how much the interests of workers and their organizations are linked. A company that cannot compete successfully will cease to exist, and its workers will lose their jobs. And the loss of a job means much more psychologically than just the loss of a paycheck. It can have devastating effects on the worker's self-esteem, the integrity and functioning of the worker's family, and the social fabric of the worker's community. The link between work and health has never been more palpable.

On the other hand, the needs of workers and their organizations do not always converge. Pressures to trim costs can create considerable stress for workers. The declining purchasing power of the American paycheck has made the two wage-earner family the rule rather than the exception. As this has occurred, pressures on both business organizations and their employees have further increased. Thus, the challenge today is to find ways of promoting worker health *and* organizational effectiveness.

As discussed in Chapter 1, the purpose of this book is: (a) to examine the problem of how to improve organizational effectiveness while maintaining a psychologically healthy environment for the work force, and (b) to explore ways in which applied psychology can begin to help both workers and their organizations to solve the many pressing human resource problems that are emerging from the new dynamics of corporate competitiveness.

The book's topics are systematically addressed in three thematic sections, Parts II through IV (Chapters 3 through 9). Each section contains two or three chapters on particular interrelated topics. Each chapter is written by a prominent author with an outstanding record of accomplishment in both organizational scholarship and practice in the topic area.

While each author was asked to address the issue of organizational competitiveness and worker welfare from the perspective of a particular topic, each was also asked to keep in mind the same six questions, to aid in providing linkages and common themes among the different perspectives. These questions include the following:

1. What historical, psychological, economic, cultural, and technological forces are contributing to the current pressures for increased competitiveness?
2. How are competitiveness pressures affecting corporate functioning?
3. How are competitiveness pressures affecting the psychological well-being of workers, their families, and their communities?
4. How can individual organizations be redesigned to increase their competitiveness while minimizing strain on employees?
5. What are the implications of these changes for the development of effective managers to fill new organizational roles?
6. What governmental initiatives are needed to increase organizational competitiveness while reducing the psychological costs?

The Structure and Content of Parts II through IV

The organization of Parts II through IV is outlined in the flow chart of forces and reactions presented in Figure 2.1. A summary of the chapters and their interrelationships in the flow chart is given below.

Part II: Historical, Social, and Technological Perspectives on the New Realities of Work and Workers

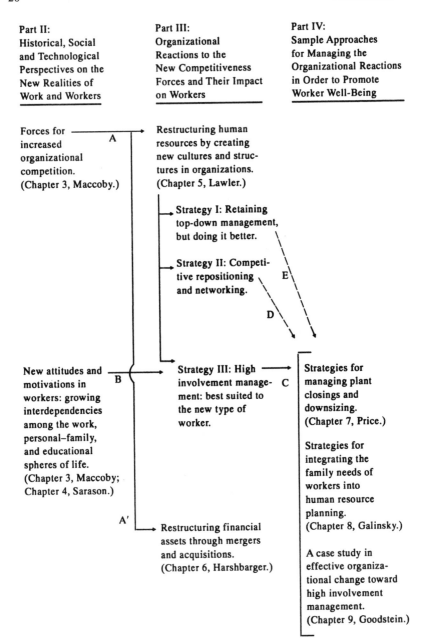

Figure 2.1 Outline of the Main Body of the Book

Chapter 3: Forces for increased organizational competition

In this chapter, Michael Maccoby begins by developing the concept of *organizational competency*, which is an organization's capacity to create the behaviors necessary for success. These competencies include not only the competencies of individual employees, but also the organization's resources, such as its technology and its practices, including how tasks are structured and how people are rewarded. Maccoby next examines increasing pressures for competition among U.S. corporations. Maccoby argues that to a significant degree these pressures come from the changing nature of the products and services created by businesses. More and more these involve a high degree of information technology, which allows them to be tailored to particular customer needs as dictated by the market. Maccoby coins the term *technoservice* to identify the type of organizational competency needed to create these new products and services, and he contrasts this paradigm with the traditional one of industrial bureaucracy. In part, a technoservice corporation is characterized by

> networks and teams; flexible work roles with authority based on competence and knowledge; flat hierarchy, front-line freedom and responsibility to make decisions to satisfy customers and adapt to different conditions; work measurements based on customer satisfaction and profitability; management as strategic planning; and leadership that develops a motivating corporate culture which supports teamwork (Chapter 3, p. 21).

Maccoby views industrial bureaucracy and technoservice as end points on a continuum. He conceptualizes this continuum as embedded in an organizational map with two directions: the horizontal (or east-west) axis represents the nature of the product or service, from standardized to customized; while the vertical (or north-south) axis reflects the type of productivity process, from "low tech" electromechanical technology to "high tech" electronic, computerized systems.

Chapters 3 and 4: New attitudes and motivations in workers

In Chapter 3, Maccoby also considers the recent changes in the motivation and values of workers. He distinguishes the older value system of the *expert*, which characterizes most corporate leaders today, from that of *helpers* and *self-developers*, the latter of which characterizes many college students today. Experts value measurable achieve-

ment and seek autonomy for themselves and control over their subordinates. In contrast, helpers value good relationships; while self-developers value a balance among work, family life, and recreation, and they
seek continual learning to insure their marketability and develop themselves as "whole persons."

Maccoby concludes by discussing how the helper and self-developer
are potentially better suited to the technoservice world than are the
experts. For example, helpers focus on good working relationships, and
self-developers value collaborative problem solving, both important
aspects of technoservice organizations.

In Chapter 4, Seymour Sarason focuses in a detailed and phenomenological manner upon the personal values and perceptions of contemporary workers, elaborating upon the dynamics of Maccoby's self-
developer. Sarason discusses the continuing breakdown since World
War II of the traditional separation among the work, personal-family,
and educational domains of life. This has been precipitated in part
by many groups who are redefining themselves and the relationships
among their working, personal and social lives—groups such as blacks
and other minorities, women, the elderly, the handicapped, gays, nurses,
and public school teachers. Out of this process emerge new expectations
from workers about personally relevant benefits, such as maternity
leave, day care, comparable pay for women, help in caring for sick or
elderly family members, wellness programs, and wheelchair-accessible
facilities.

The growing interweaving of working, personal, and social life is
also resulting, argues Sarason, in new interdependencies between private business and public education. Sarason bemoans the "great waste"
of our past public education efforts and argues for the synergistic
potential of locating some public education programs in corporate and
small business work sites. Sarason points out that this intermixing of
work and education is already taking place in the large and growing
programs corporations have taken on to educate and train their employees, from upgrading the basic math and language skills of blue-collar
workers through training programs for upper level managers.

**Part III: Organizational Reactions to the New Competitiveness Forces
and Their Impact on Workers**

Chapter 5: Restructuring human resources by creating new cultures and structures in organizations

In this chapter, Edward Lawler describes one response (see arrow A in Figure 2.1) to organizational competition: restructuring the human resources of the organization in one of three types of ways. Strategy I involves *doing the old better*, that is, trying to bring up to date the traditional industrial bureaucracy Maccoby discusses. Strategy I sticks with the traditional top-down management style, and simply puts more pressure on employees to operate more effectively, control costs, and make their organization more efficient. It is sometimes combined with an emphasis on quality and supported by *parallel participation* processes such as quality circles. Overall, Lawler's assessment is that this strategy is likely to produce only limited gains and relatively quick fixes.

Lawler's Strategy II emphasizes repositioning corporate assets and forming alliances and networks. This strategy directs a corporation to go wherever in the country or the world a particular task can be carried out. It involves forming strategic alliances with foreign partners so that each organization can do what it does well. This strategy is likely to be relatively successful, although it is limited in terms of the type of industries in which it can work.

Finally, Lawler's Strategy III involves moving to a *high involvement management* paradigm. In this type of management model, information, knowledge, rewards, and power are pushed to the lowest level in the organization in the hope of producing a more motivating work environment and reducing the dysfunctions of extremely hierarchical organizations. While this approach has only been tried by a limited number of organizations, the results are very promising, although the model also is limited to certain kinds of industries, and clearly does not fit all employees and managers.

Overall, Lawler's distinction between Strategy I versus Strategies II and III is similar to Maccoby's distinction between industrial bureaucracy and technoservice. Like Maccoby, Lawler predicts that Strategies II and III represent the wave of the future if organizations are to stay competitive. However, Lawler points out that as far as American workers are involved, Strategy II is problematic. Even though it appears to have a good potential for being competitive in the future marketplace, it raises questions about what type of work will be left in the U.S. for individuals with low education levels and low desires for involvement and challenging jobs. These individuals will not have a role in organizations which strategically position themselves around the world based on local conditions, that is, where simple repetitive work can be done for the lowest labor cost. Lawler thus concludes that Strategy III, high involvement management, has the biggest potential for transforming American businesses hiring American workers to stay competitive in today's and tomorrow's marketplaces.

As reflected in Figure 2.1 by arrow B, the new type of worker discussed by Sarason—what Maccoby describes as the self-developer—is particularly suited to Lawler's high involvement management culture. Thus it appears that organizational changes created in reaction to the new dynamics of organizational competition are moving in the same direction as psychological and social changes in worker attitudes and motivation. In other words, there is reason to believe that a particularly effective way of meeting the demands of increased organizational competitiveness—that is, Lawler's Strategy III—produces exactly the type of corporate environment that the new type of worker is personally seeking.

Chapter 6: Restructuring financial assets through mergers and acquisitions

In this chapter, Dwight Harshbarger describes an alternative organizational response (see arrow A' in Figure 2.1) to corporate competition: the restructuring of financial assets by merger and acquisition. While these events have traditionally involved abrupt layoffs and downsizing that typically have devastating effects on individual workers and managers, as Harshbarger has personally experienced, he argues that these events should not be viewed as a human resource evil to be eradicated, but rather as a new reality for which we must develop new human resource responses. He discusses how the psychosocial upheavals of the merger and acquisition process can be managed more effectively by careful planning based upon an analysis of our growing body of experience with this phenomenon.

Specifically, Harshbarger argues for two types of approaches for dealing with the new realities of mergers and acquisitions. The first approach is from the perspective of the well-being and professional contribution of the manager who is terminated due to a merger and acquisition. Harshbarger proposes that such a manager can be prepared for this change by working in *competence building environments*—corporate settings with high involvement management characteristics in which an important focus is upon developing the skills and knowledge of individual workers and managers. Involvement in such an environment will lead to the development of employees who have the personal and occupational resilience and competence to move quickly and effectively to new jobs in new organizations if a merger or acquisition in their old organization dictates this.

Harshbarger's second approach is from the perspective of the organization. If the organization is to be prepared for major changes in its organizational structure and identity through mergers and acquisitions, it needs a formal succession-planning process with at least three elements: an annual performance review of present managers; accountable programs of management development; and a program for identifying the company's future leadership based upon these prior two elements.

Part IV: Sample Approaches for Managing the Organizational Reactions in Order to Promote Worker Well-Being

In the context of corporate efforts to become more competitive, Part IV looks at sample ways in which corporations can manage the human resource ramifications of these efforts in a manner so as to reduce worker stress and, where possible, to promote worker well-being, on the one hand, while at the same time enhancing the organization's capacity to compete. In Chapter 7, Richard Price looks at strategies to accomplish these goals in the management of plant closings and downsizing. These strategies are in part an elaboration of those proposed by Harshbarger in Chapter 6 for dealing with the abrupt and frequently traumatic downsizing typically associated with a merger or acquisition. In Chapter 8, Ellen Galinsky discusses corporate efforts to integrate the family-related needs of workers into overall human resource policies. Finally, in Chapter 9, Goodstein provides a case example of how one corporation—British Airways—transformed itself from a traditional, centralized bureaucracy into a high-involvement type of organization, and how this reaped benefits for both organizational competitiveness and worker well-being.

In Figure 2.1, arrow C between Lawler's high involvement management and Chapters 7 through 9 represents the fact that the conceptual frameworks and practices discussed in these chapters are particularly suited to organizational environments with a strong high-involvement culture. However, it is possible to adapt some of these practices to enhance effectiveness in Strategy I and II organizations, and this potential is indicated by the dashed arrows D and E in Figure 2.1. Each of the chapters in Part IV are discussed below.

Chapter 7: Managing plant closings and downsizing

In this chapter, Price describes multiple negative outcomes that frequently accompany traditionally conducted plant closings, that is, plant closings that take place in the organizational mind-set of Maccoby's industrial bureaucracy and Lawler's Strategy I. Price illustrates his discussion with an actual case in which he was hired by lawyers retained by the laid-off workers to interview the workers and learn what the plant closing had meant for them and their families. Price discusses how, in the process of closing, relocation, or consolidation, decisions are made that can dramatically affect both the economic and psychological well-being of managers, workers, and community members. While it would appear that there are substantial incentives to minimize corporate costs by closing a plant rapidly with as little communication to workers, unions, and the community as possible, this can be a costly plan in the long run. Such an approach can bring unwanted legal sanctions on the corporation, prolong costly payment of unemployment benefits, and incur a variety of other hidden costs that can and should be avoided.

Based upon the many problems that have emerged with traditionally conducted closings and upon selected incidences in which these were avoided through systematic, problem-preventive planning, Price lays out a number of guidelines for how human resource managers can more effectively manage this very important event in the corporate life cycle. For example, he points out that there is a continuum of strategies and tactics for work force reduction, from natural attrition to early retirement incentives, to involuntary part-time schedules, to layoff with outplacement assistance, to layoff without outplacement assistance. These are inversely related, such that the more the short-term cost savings for the organization, the less the protection of the workers' well-being. Having this continuum as a planning tool sensitizes the human resource manager to the variety of alternative plans that are possible and to weigh the pros and cons of each within the context of the specific business situation.

Price concludes with an argument for retraining as the most future-oriented and preventive strategy for both the organization and the individual. Such retraining prevents worker obsolescence, provides the organization with a labor force that can adapt to changing and increasingly sophisticated technologies, and arms workers with skills and confidence for gaining new jobs after they have lost their old ones due to work force reduction.

Chapter 8. Integrating the family needs of workers into human resource planning

In this chapter, Galinsky reviews two types of business initiatives to support the needs of children and families: the encouragement of more preschool education, and new programs for integrating work and family responsibilities. Throughout this chapter Galinsky posits that such "family-friendly" policies and programs not be viewed as company operating expenses, but rather as "investment in human capital," and she argues that such investment in some ways "makes better business sense than an investment in capital equipment and is absolutely necessary in a time of severe competitive pressure from a global economy."

Galinsky begins the chapter with a review of recent initiatives at the federal level to expand preschool education. Business has strongly supported these efforts, but Galinsky points out a number of potential pitfalls implicit in this view: concentrating on schooling and ignoring the child care needs of employed parents; concentrating on increasing the supply of programs while giving less attention to program quality; ignoring the staffing crisis in early childhood programs; not providing comprehensive services in preschools; and focusing on preschools while ignoring other ages.

In the second part of the chapter, Galinsky reviews the development in companies of work/family initiatives. As a context to her discussion, Galinsky documents the change in demography of today's labor force—the increase in the labor force's proportion of women, dual wage-earner families, single-parent families, minorities, and older workers. She then discusses some of the new types of company human resource policies that are evolving in reaction to these demographic changes—flexible work arrangements, such as flexitime and flexiplace; maternity and paternity leave; health benefits tailored to the diverse needs of the individual worker; dependent care policies; and employee assistance and wellness programs.

Galinsky next considers organizational factors that appear to facilitate or inhibit the effective development of these new human resource initiatives in a particular corporation, and she follows this by a review of the growing evidence which documents that work/family initiatives have a payoff in increased productivity. She then goes on to discuss the importance of linking job improvement efforts, such as Quality Circles and Quality of Worklife programs, with initiatives to enhance the linkage between work and family. For example, she discusses the great potential the supervisor-supervisee relationship has for mediating between job conditions and an employee's family and personal life.

Galinsky concludes that many companies face a decision between two types of approaches for meeting competitive pressures. One is a strategy that views human resource expenses as an operating cost and proposes to become more competitive by such practices as cutting employee benefits, downsizing, and becoming "lean and mean." The other strategy views human resource expenses as a financial investment and proposes to develop and institutionalize work/family programs on the basis of their payoff for increasing a company's productivity and profitability.

Chapter 9. A case study in effective organizational change toward high involvement management

In this chapter, Goodstein discusses the social psychological theory behind organizational development (OD) consultation, a technology which can help an organization to change from the industrial bureaucracy and Strategy I paradigm of management to a technoservice and Strategy II or III type of model. This discussion forms the conceptual framework for Goodstein's description of his work as an OD consultant with British Airways to effect this type of change.

Goodstein views an organization as an open social system, which emphasizes that it takes in resources (information, raw materials, human resources, and so on) from the outside environment and works to transform them into desired products or services that are then exported back into the environment. Max Weber's (1924/1947) famous concept of "bureaucracy," the type of organization Maccoby calls an industrial bureaucracy and Lawler calls a top-down organization, is viewed as a *closed system* characterized by impersonality and rationality—"where rules cover all contingencies; where technically expert supervisors act as impartial autocrats; and where communications follow a carefully controlled, hierarchical path." In contrast, the type of corporation Maccoby calls technoservice and Lawler calls high involvement management is viewed as an *open system*, characterized by being a "flexible, porous, and adaptive" organization which is "guided by its vision and values rather than rules" and in which "communications are open, and boundaries are readily permeable, both internally and externally."

Parallelling Maccoby's view of the move in American business from industrial bureaucracy to technoservice and Lawler's view of a move from top-down to high-involvement organizations, Goodstein sees American corporations changing their image of the organization and its members as machine and parts to one of "a nested set of open, living systems and subsystems dependent upon the larger environment for survival" (Waldbaum, 1987, p. 19).

In the second part of his chapter, Goodstein presents the British Airways (BA) case study from his perspective as an OD consultant. In this role, he has dealt with the total organization, using such approaches as organizational assessment via interviews and questionnaires to clarify problems and plan change programs, team building to enhance working relationships among employees, and process consultation to examine the pattern of communication at BA. Goodstein differentiates nine types of activities involved in the BA change effort. Each of these is defined in terms of two dimensions: whether the activities are directed at changing individual employees, organizational structures, or organizational culture and climate; and whether the activities are directed at unfreezing the old bureaucratic practices, at movement toward the new high-involvement practices, or refreezing newly established high-involvement practices.

In the final part of the chapter, Goodstein discusses the important concept of organizational culture, which can be described behaviorally as "the way we do things around here" and ideationally as the basic beliefs an organization's members hold regarding human nature and "the way things ought to be." Goodstein's discussion links with and expands upon those of Maccoby and Lawler about this important topic.

Goodstein discusses the importance for organizational effectiveness of active managing of clashes in corporate culture so as to reduce their destabilizing and disruptive effects. Goodstein considers three types of such culture conflicts: (a) those that can occur between two or more parts of a presently established organization; (b) those that can occur when two previously independent organizations come together through a process of corporate merger or acquisition; and (c) those that occur when a corporation in one national culture expands its operations into a country with a different national culture (as when the Japanese company of Kawasaki Motors developed a new plant operation in Nebraska).

In the context of this latter, transnational type of cultural conflict, Goodstein considers recent discussions in the media and in management circles of the need for American industry to adopt Japanese management practices. Goodstein points out the naiveté of doing this from a corporate culture perspective; for the management practices developed by the Japanese work well because of the match between these practices and the traditional Japanese culture, a culture which contrasts with American culture in being less egalitarian, less pluralistic, less open, and less individualistic.

In closing this chapter, Goodstein concludes that managers must contend with the external pressures that require organizational changes and the internal resistance to such changes. Effective change management requires balancing these opposing forces, while retaining the momentum to move from the present state, through a transition state, to a desired future state.

Viewing the Issues from Multiple Disciplinary and Stylistic Perspectives

In deciding on authors for the different chapters, the editors deliberately chose individuals with different professional roles, presentation styles, and disciplinary backgrounds. This was done in the belief that the authors' different disciplinary and stylistic perspectives—that is, their different mind-sets and ways of selecting and presenting material on a particular issue—are an important cross-cutting dimension in gaining a broad understanding of the substantive issues.

In terms of roles, Chapter 1 is written by Radigan, a senior human resource manager who has devoted his entire career to this role. The other chapters are written by professional psychologists who have held positions not only as academic psychologists, but also as organizational consultants. In addition, two of these authors—Harshbarger and Goodstein—were full-time senior corporate executives when they wrote their chapters; another, Maccoby, has a disciplinary background in anthropology and psychoanalysis.

In terms of perspectives, the different approaches taken by the various authors represent different facets of the reality of corporate attempts to adapt to the new competitiveness pressures of the marketplace. For example, the different chapters take such diverse perspectives as:

- the phenomenological experience of the professional manager (Sarason, Harshbarger) or the laid-off worker (Price);
- the demographics of the changing work force (Radigan, Galinsky);
- the exposition of existent formal organizational theory, such as the concepts of open social systems and corporate culture (Goodstein, Harshbarger);
- the development of new theoretical concepts, such as technoservice (Maccoby) and the high involvement organization (Lawler);
- the description of detailed, practical case studies in action research in which the author has been a participant observer, with resultant suggested guidelines for the practice of human resource management (Price, Goodstein); and
- the exploration of a set of issues—business's adoption of pro-family and pro-education positions—from the perspective of national policy formation (Galinsky).

Chapter 10, which concludes the book, begins with a recapitulation of Chapters 1 through 9 and then discusses two main overarching themes which develop across these chapters: emerging interdependencies and synergies among individual, organizational, and societal wellbeing.

References

Waldbaum, P. (1987, July 24). Motivate or alienate? Firms hire gurus to change their "cultures." *The Wall Street Journal*, p. 19.

Weber, M. (1947). *The theory of social and economic organization* (A. M. Henderson & T. Parsons, Trans.). New York: Oxford University Press. (Original work published 1924)

PART II

Historical, Social, and Technological Perspectives on the New Realities of Work and Workers

3 Forces for Increased Organizational Competition: Implications for Leadership and Organizational Competence

MICHAEL MACCOBY

Over the past 30 years, I have been studying the question of what makes people productive in peasant villages, factories, offices, and high technology laboratories in the United States, Great Britain, Scandinavia, the Soviet Union, and Japan. This question can be divided into two parts: what motivates people; and what empowers them? The answers vary in different societies, with different cultural values and technology. In every society, the most productive people are those with a deep interest in their work. They are people who ask, "Why are we doing this?" as well as "Can we do it better?" They seek knowledge to eliminate waste and improve the quality of products and services. They combine hard work with high standards and care for the land, animals, tools, and people. For the most productive farmers, bricklayers, engineers, entrepreneurs, and doctors, work is a means not only of making a living, but also of self-expression and contribution to society. Throughout history, however, changes in technology and work have forced people to adapt, sometimes with considerable human cost.

What distinguishes the world of work in modern society from that of the traditional peasant village are the technology and organization that enable or empower the individual worker. The peasant uses simple tools: the hoe, rake, shovel, and plow. He works alone or with his family. His values are strongly individualistic. His experience with the uncertainties of the weather make him hoard against possible catastrophe, and he tends to be conservative, even stingy. He is suspicious of people he has not known for years. He has learned that middlemen and gov-

ernment representatives from the city may exploit him (Fromm &
Maccoby, 1970). In contrast, workers today must use all kinds of
complex tools. In large, technology-based organizations, not only do
people have to work cooperatively with co-workers but also with
customers and suppliers. Experts must be open-minded and emotionally
generous, if they are to combine their knowledge productively. They
require skills in group problem solving as well as technical expertise.
They must be able to follow as well as lead.

Organizational Competency

In the modern world, organization itself is a tool that creates power;
and conversely, individual empowerment depends on organizational
competencies. It is useful to think about organizational competencies,
especially because people tend to think that individual skills alone will
create a successful organization. This is not the case.

I define *organizational competencies* as the organizational capabilities that create the behaviors necessary for success. These competencies
in turn depend not only on *individual competencies*, but also on resources, such as technology and organizational practices and measurements, including how tasks are structured, what is measured, and how
people are rewarded. To take a rather simple example, consider the
organizational competencies necessary for a baseball team to win.
These are the competencies of offense (producing runs) and defense
(pitching and fielding). For offense, a team must be able to get a player
on base and from first to home using sacrifices, hits-and-runs, etc. The
team must be able to score against both left- and right-handed pitching.
For defense, a team must be able to execute double plays, throw runners
out, position themselves for different batters in different situations, and
so on. These organizational competencies require not only individual
skills such as batting, pitching, and fielding skill, but also knowledge
of the rules and experience about what works, when to improvise, how
to take advantage of opponents' errors, etc. Leadership competencies
are also essential: strategy, communication, decision making during the
game, coaching, motivating, resolving conflicts, and selecting talent.
Constructive criticism must be encouraged.

Organizational competency also demands that individuals practice
values of teamwork: cooperation, supportiveness, self-sacrifice, and
followership. A good hitter who thinks only of his own average and not

the team diminishes organizational competency. However, if a hitter is told to sacrifice, yet his salary is based on hitting home runs and there is no measure of successful sacrifices, the contradiction will undermine organizational competency. The values needed must be the ones measured and rewarded. The final element of resources includes technology (bats, gloves, field in good shape), money to pay players, and a farm club system to develop replacements.

In the same way, we might examine organizational competencies of the military (from the discipline of the Roman phalanx to the interdependency and communication of the Strategic Air Command), factories (from the standardization of Adam Smith's pin producers to the adaptability of computerized Flexible Manufacturing Systems), and service organizations (from the reliability of garbage collection to the customization of complex financial services). To reach their goals, all of these organizations must develop different competencies.

During the past few years the requirements for organizational competence for international competition have become more demanding, and this challenges traditional values and ways of thinking. Consider the car industry. The Toyota production system dramatically increased quality and reduced waste. The Honda approach to product design cut product cycles from five to three years. Auto producers in the U.S. and Europe have struggled to meet these standards. Much of the conflict that occurs today in large American companies is provoked by the pressure to develop the competencies required by the market and technology. Organizational forms and individual styles that worked well in the past are inadequate.

The Industrial Bureaucracy

Twenty years ago there seemed to be an extremely effective organizational form, the industrial bureaucracy, organized to produce standardized outputs with uniform roles (Weber, 1924/1947). The logic of this organization is that lower level jobs should be as simplified as possible, coordinated and controlled by the next level up. Productivity is improved by lowering labor costs through rationalization and automation. The dominant theory of F. W. Taylor (1911) proposed that there was "one best way" of designing work and this could be determined by scientific methods. This organizational form proved fabulously successful, especially for the United States in an era in which American industry controlled world markets.

However, it was criticized from a humanistic point of view. Even Adam Smith was concerned about the negative human effects of division of labor and work simplification. Narrow, fragmented jobs stunt intellectual development. They also depress morale and productive motivation in people capable of doing more. Experiments at the Western Electric Hawthorne plant in the late 1920s showed that when managers implemented workers' ideas about how to do the work, productivity improved (Roethlisberger & Dickson, 1939). Indeed, the mere fact of researchers paying attention to workers facilitated productivity increases, the so-called "Hawthorne effect."

In 1972, I began a participative work improvement project at Harman Industries in Bolivar, Tennessee. This work carried the Hawthorne approach a step further by involving a union, the United Auto Workers, and training workers to take on some management functions (Maccoby, 1981).

The success of the Bolivar experiment stimulated Quality of Worklife (QWL) projects at General Motors (GM) and American Telephone and Telegraph (AT&T). These programs, designed to foster human growth and to improve organizational effectiveness, consist of labor-management committees that are set up to evaluate the work environment in an organization and develop initiatives for alleviating conditions that have an adverse effect on employee well-being. QWL programs usually include many different practices, such as participative decision making, job enrichment, improved safety and working conditions, and compensation programs that emphasize gainsharing (Hackman, 1977).

A related development has been the growth of quality techniques, including "Quality Circles" (QCs). In the late 1940s, Edward Deming, an American, lectured in Japan about statistical methods for quality control. Deming emphasized that production quality must involve both workers and management; and the Japanese combined these ideas with a philosophy of bringing workers together in groups to solve problems. At the core of the Japanese program was the assumption that the worker who performs a job is the one who best knows how to identify problems, but it is the responsibility of management to use this information to improve systems. (It should be noted that the Japanese quality approach is much more than Quality Circles and includes the whole "pull-versus-push" system, starting with the customer and including "just-in-time" delivery, low inventory, multiskilled training, and supervisors in teaching roles.)

By the 1970s, when Japanese products became synonymous with product quality and technological advancement, American corporations went over to Japan to study their practices and quickly adopted the idea of Quality Circles. These basically consist of groups of employees who meet on a regular basis to discuss ways of modifying work procedures in order to improve production. Although QCs were not explicitly developed to enhance employee morale, growth, and commitment, they often have this effect (Marks, 1986; Ouchi, 1981).

However, in actual practice, although QWL and QC projects improved both productivity and morale, throughout the 1970s and 1980s they tended to remain encapsulated, limited to plants led by visionary managers. Often, management did not make use of employee ideas.

The reason for this was that the QWL approach to worker participation was not necessary for the success of most companies. The bureaucratic industrial organization was good enough as measured by the bottom line. Furthermore, the natural evolution of QWL into flexible project teams threatened both the formal and informal structure of traditional organizations. At both lower and higher levels, employees resisted bureaucratic regimentation. At lower levels, unions gained some control for workers over their work by bargaining contracts that delineated an exact job description. As a result, management was stuck with numerous job titles that limited their flexibility in using workers. Although this depressed productivity, the market continued to pay the price. At higher levels, managers built walls around their turf and resisted cross-functional projects that might limit their control.

The Challenge to Industrial Bureaucracy

What challenged the traditional industrial bureaucracy and called for new organizational competencies were, first, new competencies developed by the Japanese; then changes in the products demanded by the market and the production processes created by computerization. In electronics and chemicals as well as automobiles, increased competition required not only higher levels of productivity, but also faster product cycles and levels of quality not achieved by the standard organization. Large customers demanded customized information-telecommunications systems and applications. As simpler jobs were automated, those that remained required greater intellectual and interpersonal skills from both managers and workers. The logic of simplified, fragmented jobs no longer worked. The functional hierarchies proved unwieldy, costly and dangerous. The traditional industrial bureaucratic organization lacked the competencies required to succeed.

Attempting to adapt, managers began to experiment with new organizational forms, some of which had been tried out by innovators over the past twenty years. These included flatter organizations, so-called inverted pyramids, self-managed teams and so on. In these organizations, authority was delegated, workers were cross-trained, and teams learned to solve problems and innovate. In some cases, such as Volvo's Kalmar auto assembly plant, opened in 1974, the production technology was redesigned to allow workers more opportunity for high quality craftsmanship, a step which Volvo's CEO, P. G. Gyllenhammar, considered essential for market success. (In 1989, Volvo inaugurated its assembly plant at Uddevalla, which goes even further in creating self-management teams of workers.)

Some of these organizational developments were impelled by the egalitarian ideology of the 1960s, such as the Norwegian Industrial Democracy Project, which spread the idea of self-managed, semiautonomous teams. Others, under the heading of sociotechnical development, proposed similar methods of optimizing both technical efficiency and satisfying, meaningful work that allowed opportunity for growth and career development. Still others, under the increasingly popular banner of the "Quality Movement," began to focus on the company-customer interface and used the concept of external and internal customers as a lever to transform the organization.

In sum, by the 1990s, for many companies to maintain organizational competency, they will have to change their management model from industrial bureaucracy to a new paradigm, which I call *technoservice* and define as

> the use of systematic knowledge and information-communications technology for the benefit of customers and clients. . . . Technoservice is characterized by customizing products and services for customers and clients both internal and external to the organization. Technoservice organization is characterized by networks and teams; flexible work roles with authority based on competence and knowledge; flat hierarchy, front-line freedom and responsibility to make decisions to satisfy customers and adapt to different conditions; work measurements based on customer satisfaction and profit-

ability; management as strategic planning; and leadership that develops a motivating corporate culture which supports teamwork. (Maccoby, 1988, p. 21)

The Organizational Map

For managers aware that they must improve organizational competency, these different approaches are often confusing. Many managers, trained in bureaucratic-industrial logic, seek a new "one best way" to organize work. They have taken Quality Circle approaches developed in Japanese factories and tried to apply them directly to technoservice work, with limited success. My experience in the workplace is that different organizational competencies are required by different types of products and processes.

I have tried to make sense of all these various approaches to change by proposing an organizational map based on two dimensions having to do with product and production process, as shown in Table 3.1. The horizontal or east-west axis represents the nature of the product and service, from standardized to customized. The vertical or north-south axis represents the type of production process, from electromechanical technology to electronic, computerized systems. The traditional industrial bureaucracy is found in the lower left or southwest corner of the map. This is the world of standardized products, economies of scale, and Tayloristic scientific management.

As we move up diagonally in a northwest direction, the product may remain standardized, but the process becomes automated, as in the continuous process of paper and pulp mills, breweries, and oil refineries. Here the traditional bureaucratic organization becomes dangerous as well as unproductive. Unless workers on the front line have knowledge and authority, accidents happen, as in the Three Mile Island nuclear plant near-meltdown, or the North Sea Bravo blowout. At Three Mile Island, everyone followed instructions, but the bureaucratic industrial book did not give the training and authority they needed to close a valve and avoid an accident. Some of the best-known work innovations of the 1970s, such as the General Goods Plan in Topeka, Kansas, created organizations appropriate for continuous process technology. Researchers found that self-managed teams of workers who were broadly trained used the technology more productively as measured by higher quality, less product loss, and less downtime for equipment.

TABLE 3.1 From Industrial Bureaucracy to Technoservice:
An Organization Map

	"High Tech" (north)	Computerized Manufacturing		Technoservice
		northwest quadrant	northeast quadrant	
Automation (process)		southwest quadrant	southeast quadrant	
	"Low Tech" (south)	Industrial Bureaucracy		Personal Service
		Standardized (west)		Customized (east)

Customization
(product)

Moving to the east side of the map, we enter the world of customization. The service organization is in the southeast. Traditionally, it involves store clerks, bank tellers, and airline cabin attendants. However, as we move up the map, going north, we enter a zone in which organizational competence requires using computers to satisfy customer requests for responsive services. Unlike the industrial bureaucracies, where workers must repeat the same tasks, the technoservice organization requires front-line employees who customize their responses and vary their behavior according to changing circumstances.

In the northeast corner of the map, where companies produce customized data and telecommunications systems for large customers, organizational competency requires integrating teams of experts from marketing, production, development engineering, and operations who must work in partnership with the customer whose technology and product are very different. New organizational roles and measurements are needed. The bureaucratic-industrial logic becomes seriously misleading.

There are different, key organizational competencies associated with each of the four quadrants of the map. In the southwest quadrant, the domain of industrial bureaucracy, it is the continual improvement gained by the Japanese "humanware" approach to high quality and cost reduction. In the northwest quadrant, the domain of computerized manufacturing, it is delegated control of automated systems, educating front-line teams to maintain machinery and avoid loss. In the southeast quadrant, it is the inverted pyramid with an empowered front line of service technicians or financial clerks who implement a common strategy. This calls for investments in training, communication of objectives, leadership skills, resources and freedom to do the job, and use of Quality Circles and Quality of Worklife processes to improve systems and relationships. Finally, the northeast quadrant, the domain of technoservice, calls for competencies of cross-functional expert teams with the customer as partner. In a timely way, these teams must be able to produce applications that improve the customer's organizational competencies.

Each of the four boxes in Table 3.1 is associated with a different type of appropriate teamwork. In the southwest box of industrial bureaucracy, it is the hierarchically structured team, with a manager supervising two or more supervisees, with each of the supervisees in turn managing two or more individuals organizationally below them, and so forth. This arrangement is sometimes supplemented by cross-functional Quality Circles.

In the northwest box of computerized manufacturing, a multiskilled, nonhierarchical, self-managed team directly controls the technology. The team leader functions in the roles of facilitator and coach.

In the southeast box of personal service, self-managed teams relate to customers and are coordinated by managers who again act as coach-facilitators.

Finally, in the northeast box of technoservice, the team is structured as a *heterarchy* rather than a hierarchy, which means that leadership shifts according to who has the knowledge needed.

Many companies pursue a strategy of technoservice, moving from producing standardized products to customized solutions. (A notable example cited in *Why Work* [Maccoby, 1988] is Westinghouse Furniture Systems, which was transformed from a losing to a profitable company by this change in strategy.) However, many large companies manage work that is all over the organizational map. For example, AT&T has assembly-line manufacturing in the southwest quadrant and flexible manufacturing systems in the northwest quadrant. The financial services of America Transtech are in the southeast corner, with customized data networking for large business customers in the northeast corner. Each of these calls for different organizational competencies. Managers must recognize they are not in a world of either/or (like McGregor's [1960] Theory X versus Theory Y), but of multiple competencies and organizational forms. The project team in the northeast quadrant still requires functional maintenance organizations to recruit and develop the experts who will produce in cross-functional teams.

The more companies move products and processes to the northeast quadrant, the more they are selling *solutions* and *values* rather than standardized products. When AT&T and IBM sell customized systems, they are able to charge a premium because customers want the prestige of high quality and the sense of security promised by good service. The belief by customers that companies can deliver these values has been called *market capital*. This market capital is increased or decreased according to organizational competence.

Employees at AT&T, IBM, and other companies that sell these values must not only have technical skills; they must also understand customers' business needs and internalize values of quality and service. Individual front-line service workers must be empowered to make quick decisions to satisfy customers. Inevitably they will make mistakes; these must be used to learn. Punishment will kill risk taking and undermine empowerment. Strategists at the top must listen to fresh information about competitors from the front lines. It needs to be emphasized that technical and business knowledge are not enough. Organizational competency requires communication of objectives, interpersonal skills of coaching and communication, measurements that reinforce customer service, and rewards that encourage cross-functional teamwork. Unless employees are motivated to provide quality and service, a company's market capital will diminish.

Leadership, Motivation and Values

When we think about motivation of front-line workers, we tend to do so within the bureaucratic-industrial logic. We think about people using only parts of themselves, partial persons who must be motivated to do the same simplified task over and over again. This standardized partial person is to be motivated by a standardized motivator—money. However, once organizational competency requires more complex behavior, and once more of the whole person is needed at work, traditional theories of motivation prove inadequate. For employees to care about the business and achieve higher levels of trust and teamwork, management must understand the values they bring to work. There must be respect for individual dignity, and work must be meaningful. As business customizes its products and services, so must it customize its management of people.

It is hard for many managers who have grown up and been rewarded for success in the industrial bureaucracies to change. They believe that what has worked in the past should work in the future.

Why Work (Maccoby, 1988) describes the results of interviewing executives of large companies in the U.S. and Sweden. Most express the "expert" profile. Oriented to individual achievement and control, their values fit neatly with the industrial bureaucracy. Brought up in families headed by a single male wage earner, their model of leadership is the good father who gives his son or daughter autonomy. Indeed, the strong drive for autonomy by expert managers causes the organizational paradox observed by Douglass Carmichael. When you ask managers at each level what would make their work more satisfying, they will usually say "more freedom" or "more autonomy." Sometimes they will expand on this: "Get the boss off my back. Give me clear goals and objectives, but let me achieve them my way." When you then ask these managers what they need in relation to subordinates, they say: "I need more control." This translates into MBO (management by objectives) for the manager and MBI (management by instructions) for subordinates. A good example of the problems this can cause is Zuboff's (1988) description of how managers in paper and pulp mills with continuous process technology resist delegating control to front-line workers.

The result: managers guard turf and organizations cannot function without internal dealmaking. (The chief of surgery at a large hospital told me he has to do three or four deals to get an operating room.)

The psychology of the expert seriously impedes the development of technoservice organizational competency. Project teams, matrix management, and strategic dialogue all make the expert uneasy. There is no clear turf, and any agreement means a loss of autonomy and control. Furthermore, experts work comfortably only with others who share their values.

I travelled to Japan with an expert manager who later said: "I know it works, but I don't like it. It doesn't feel right. Who is really in charge? What are the incentives? It all seems unclear." What experts must realize is that the bureaucratic industrial organization is hard-wired into their psyches. This keeps them from using organization as a flexible tool and from understanding others with different values.

In *Why Work*, while more than half of the employees surveyed were experts, for about one fifth, the opportunity to help people was what made work meaningful. They feel they are not usually rewarded for helping. In the technoservice economy, they are a resource which can be developed and employed to strengthen values of service, provided that leaders understand their motivation, including the importance of good relationships and appreciation for their contribution.

A growing percentage of the work force differs from experts and helpers in that the meaning of work for them involves self-development. This group comprised 20% of the more than 3000 employees that were surveyed in business and government. However, the percentage rose to 30% for people aged thirty and under and 40% for college students, and these figures underestimate the influence of self-development values. In this group are the offspring of families where both parents have careers. Their childhood experience forms work values significantly different from those of the experts. At an early age, the self-developers learn about shared authority from parents who also blur traditional male and female roles. They grow up in an atmosphere of dialogue and compromise. Sent to day care centers, they learn early on that they must get along with strangers. Indeed, many learn to manage their parents by provoking guilt, in order to secure at least some support from them. In contrast to the experts, self-developers do not expect parents to take care of them. They recognize that they must at the same time become more independent and cooperative.

Emphasis in these dual career families is on continual learning. The meaning of self-development involves maintaining one's marketability and expressing oneself at work. But this is not all. Although they enjoy the challenge and sociability of work, they recognize the need to balance work with play and family life. They seek to develop themselves as whole persons: healthy, wealthy, and having a good time. Rather than autonomy, they seek independence (or counterdependence) and leadership that facilitates teamwork, coaches them, and empowers them. Unlike the experts, they are not satisfied by paternal approval, but seek more objective measures of performance. They are most comfortable with explicit contracts that make clear what is expected of them in terms of behavior and what they in turn can expect from management.

The increase in self-developers tracks with the growing entry of women into the work force. In 1950, 70% of families were headed by sole male wage earners. Now it is less than one-third of families. Between 1980 and 1985, the percentage of women with children under three who continued to work jumped from 25 to 50.

It should be obvious that the self-developers are potentially better fitted to the technoservice world than are the experts. Self-developers enjoy the quality process, with its emphasis on problem solving and teamwork, and satisfying the customer feels natural to them. But they seek leaders who will both coach and learn with them. They are frustrated with their expert bosses who in turn view them as uncommitted, lacking loyalty and sufficient dedication to the firm. One self-developer responded: "I want to be involved, but not necessarily committed. It's like a breakfast of bacon and eggs. The hen is involved; the pig is committed."

Recently I met with AT&T managers and CWA union leaders who were strategizing about how to transform a cumbersome industrial bureaucracy and empower the front line of service technicians so they could develop the organizational competency to solve customer problems quickly and effectively. At first they focused on freedom and autonomy, but the self-developer ethic challenged this simplistic view of empowerment. To empower the front line, they decided, requires leadership that provides clear objectives, sufficient training to do the job, processes such as Quality Circle methods to improve systems and Quality of Worklife techniques to improve relationships, resources including tools and budgets, and—of course—freedom to take risks to satisfy customers. Such empowerment will not work if well-intentioned failures are punished and the bearer of bad news is shot.

The New Model of Leadership

It has been fashionable among business gurus to describe the new corporate leader as an orchestra conductor (Drucker, 1988; Sculley, 1987). These writers contrast the bureaucratic-industrial leader of the past who gives orders and expects the troops to march in lock step with a creative maestro, whose high standards, exciting vision and seductive demands shape, stretch, and discipline a group of individual experts into a high-performing team.

How useful is this metaphor? To a degree it seems to fit the case of Steve Jobs leading the Macintosh development team to realize his vision of a user-friendly desktop computer. But only to a degree. The orchestra conductor knows the score. His job is to get the experts to play according to plan. In many a complex R&D operation, the vision has not been fully written beforehand. Rather, the team has to figure out new ways to solve problems or achieve results. As we have described, business success in the southeast of the organizational map requires empowering the front line of service technicians and salespeople to use their judgment to best satisfy customers.

This is not a matter of playing by the score, but of improvising in groups. Leaders do not get results by waving batons and keeping the beat, but by educating, communicating strategy, listening, facilitating group problem solving, and coordinating with other groups—all functions that do not fit easily into the model of the expert orchestra conductor. Rather than managing tasks, increasingly leaders must manage relationships.

One of the key elements producing the success of Japanese auto companies has been their organizational competency in designing products for ease of manufacture. As Honda managers described it to me, project leaders are not orchestra conductors but facilitators and integrators. A large part of their job is to make sure everyone's knowledge is used and that the team learns from experience.

Consider an example of even more complex teamwork in the technoservice corner of the organizational map, such as AT&T marketers, development engineers, service technicians, accountants, and regulatory lawyers combining skills to create a customized data and voice network for a large customer such as a multinational corporation or state government. Here the image of orchestra conductor seems woefully inadequate. The tasks of leadership not only require organizing different functions to satisfy the customer, but also negotiating within the departments of the company to gain resources for the project. Upfront team building is essential to establish good working relationships. It is unlikely that any one person can exercise all the leadership functions required.

The problem with trying to create a model for the new leader is that the very attempt to do so tends to express bureaucratic-industrial logic that there is one best way to do things, including leading. The bureaucratic industrial leader is supposed to be the "big brain" who runs the machine, much like an orchestra conductor. In the new logic of technoservice, leadership is best conceived in terms of functions, not persons. These functions, which include business strategy, implementation, creating a climate for innovation and learning, designing organizations, building teams and alliances, coaching, and defending corporate values, including quality and service, can be carried out by a combination of different people with different styles. Instead of one best way to organize leadership, teams should figure out up front what leadership functions are required and how they will be carried out and evaluated. Unless that is done, there will likely be chaos resolved through inefficient crisis management.

In technically based companies, typically, there are work organizations all over the organizational map. In one Volvo stamping factory, there are assembly lines, automated processes, and craft shops. In the Bell Laboratories, there are breakthrough projects together with formatted development work. Unless the person in a leadership role is multicompetent, he or she is likely to feel schizophrenic moving from industrial bureaucracies to technoservice teams.

In each area of the map, there is a need for leaders who balance tough-minded strategic skills with respect for individual dignity and human understanding. There will always be room in business for exceptional innovators acting as orchestra conductors, impresarios, ringmasters and champions. But these exciting metaphors do not describe the varied roles of leadership that must be designed and practiced in complex companies.

Changing Bureaucracies

Why Work (Maccoby, 1988) describes how three companies transformed traditional industrial bureaucracies into technoservice businesses; in the process, all three became profitable. The companies—AT&T American Transtech, Westinghouse Furniture Systems, and Scandinavian Airlines—followed a similar pattern. They focused on business customers and their needs. They began to sell customized service. To create the necessary organizational competencies, they involved front-line employees in redesigning work. To support this approach, they broke down functional walls to create customer-focused projects and aligned measurements.

For most employees, these changes were liberating and empowering. For experts at middle management levels, they were threatening. In each case, after attempts at coaching, the CEOs had to remove executives. One said of a manager he had replaced:

> I respect him as an individual, but he just couldn't let go. He so had to control his department that no one else could get into it. We can only succeed here if everyone gets into everyone else's business. He has left and is now running a small company where he seems happier.

The market and new technology demand that businesses develop new competencies, and these require changes in values and leadership functions. Inevitably, some people will find it hard to adapt while others will welcome the change. Those who study organizations and are consulted by leaders have a role to play to help managers understand the organizational competencies required and the way successful companies throughout the world have developed them. Successful change requires that organizations—as well as individuals—learn, try out new approaches, and implement what works.

References

Drucker, P. (1988). The coming of the new organization. *Harvard Business Review, 66*, 45-53.

Fromm, E., & Maccoby, M. (1970). *Social character in a Mexican village.* New York: Prentice-Hall.

Hackman, J. R. (1977). Work design. In J. R. Hackman & J. L. Suttle (Eds.), *Improving life at work: Behavioral approaches to organizational change.* Santa Monica, CA: Goodyear.

Maccoby, M. (1981). *The leader: A new face for American management.* New York: Simon & Schuster.

Maccoby, M. (1988). *Why work: Leading the new generation.* New York: Simon & Schuster.

Marks, M. L. (1986). The question of quality circles. *Psychology Today, 20*, 36-47.

McGregor, D. (1960). *The human side of enterprise.* New York: McGraw-Hill.

Ouchi, W. G. (1981). *Theory Z.* Reading, MA: Addison-Wesley.

Roethlisberger, F. J., & Dickson, W. J. (1939). *Management and the worker.* Cambridge, MA: Harvard University Press.

Sculley, J. (1987). *Odyssey.* New York: Harper & Row.

Taylor, F. W. (1911). *The principles of scientific management.* New York: Harper.

Weber, M. (1947). *The theory of social and economic organization* (A. M. Henderson & T. Parsons, Trans.). New York: Oxford University Press. (Original work published in 1924)

Zuboff, S. (1988). *The age of the smart machine.* New York: Basic Books.

4 New Attitudes and Motivations in Workers: Growing Interdependencies Among the Work, Personal-Family, and Educational Spheres of Life

SEYMOUR B. SARASON

It was not until midlife that I came to see how devoid of boundaries were the different spheres of my existence. Yes, there was the private-social-family world, the world of work, and the rest of the world. But these worlds were phenomenologically like a crazy quilt, strange to the eye but nevertheless all of a piece. I, like everyone else, had labels for these worlds and could talk about them as if they were phenomenologically distinct, whereas the plain fact was that they were not. As an individual I was—in principle—in the same position as our country, struggling to comprehend and adapt to a new world in which everything seemed to be related to everything else, and no longer able to maintain the myth that it was the captain of its fate and master of its soul.

How to understand these changes and their implications for individual and social action was a question that came to interest me. If the answers I came up with are incomplete and unsatisfactory—they may also be very wrong—I have no doubt whatsoever that I am right about one thing: we are well into an era where it no longer makes personal, practical, or conceptual sense to talk about work independent of the crazy-quilt quality of contemporary life.

Breakdown of the Separation Between the
Domains of Personal and Work Life

Let me begin with an autobiographical fragment. For ten years in midlife my wife and I had to deal with four slowly dying parents. Our parents lived in New Jersey and New York. Given their condition and dependence on us, at least once a week one of us—frequently both of us—visited one set of parents. It was by no means infrequent that we would do the Connecticut-New Jersey-New York circuit in one day. At one point it became necessary to bring my father to a nursing home in New Haven; during the last two years of her life my mother-in-law had to live with us. It dawned on me one day that the one condition that made it possible for us to do what we had (and wanted) to do was that I was employed by a university. What if I had a job that required a 9-to-5 schedule? If that had been the case, what would have been the consequences for our psychological stability and our work? As a Yale professor I had a good deal of control over how I spent my time. I could, although I never had to, cancel a class and make it up at another time. My presence at faculty or committee meetings was rarely crucial. My top priority has always been writing, but if you have to change priorities and are able to, you do just that. But the truly important point is that I was in a setting in which it was taken for granted that personal crises required the setting to be supportive and flexible, indeed to bend to the needs of its members even if those needs meant temporary changes in work roles. Put in another way, the university paid more than lip service to two facts: the different worlds of each of its individual members are inextricably intertwined; and there are times when the university should and must alter its conventional obligations to those different worlds.

What is distinctive about the university is that this view of its obligations did not come about as a result of negotiations or adversarial conflict. It is a view that rests on a value judgment about what its members owe each other, what the institution owes to each of them, and what each member owes the institution. It is not a written, formulated, or articulated value. Its implicit nature becomes explicit only at times of personal crisis or tragedy. I go on the assumption that no one—at least no one I have ever talked with—would criticize the university for actions consistent with that value judgment. I have talked with people who go on to say that the university can do what it does because it can "afford" to do so, that is, it is not under pressure to show a profit; efficiency in producing a product is not its highest priority; and it is not subject to the same degree of public scrutiny and the competitive marketplace as, for example, a corporation is. As one corporate executive said to me:

> Of course we are aware that the personal and work lives of our employees are interconnected. We could be a lot more efficient and profitable if they were better interconnected. And we do try to be understanding and helpful. But we are not a social service agency, although if we gave into all of the union demands, that is what we could become. We are in the business of producing and making a profit, and to the extent that we forget that we are dead ducks.

This individual was unaware how dramatically different his view was from that of people in comparable roles 50 or more years ago in that he acknowledged three things: like it or not, the different worlds of employees were intertwined; intertwining could not, if only because of self-interest, be ignored; and his company had to respond in some ways to that intertwining, albeit reluctantly and minimally. You could say that the bad news is that he viewed his situation as a problem of constraint and interference with his primary mission. You could say that the good news is that he acknowledged that the worlds of work and non-work are inextricably intertwined in ways that he, like it or not, will be unable to ignore.

We cannot understand the changes that have taken and will continue to take place in people's phenomenology of work unless we grasp a change in worldview that occurred as a direct consequence of World War II. There are several ways of describing the change. One of those ways is captured in the phrase "great expectations." To a degree as never before—in myriads of ways, direct and indirect, explicit and implicit—the post-World War II generations were encouraged to expect a fulfilling life. That expectation has a long history in American rhetoric and ideology, but before World War II that expectation did not rest on the assumption that it was society's role to underwrite, so to speak, its realization. Such realization was an individual responsibility dependent on motivation, perseverance, frugalness, and other Horatio Alger-like virtues. You were to expect great things in life in this land of opportunity, but the responsibility to achieve the good life was an individual one. "That government is best which governs the least" was more than rhetoric. It was public policy and most people did not quarrel with it. Rugged individualism, and all that that implies, was a significant feature of the American worldview. That is what made America great, the theory went, and that is the way it should continue to be. Someone put it this way: "Certainly society should not place obstacles in the path of individuals, but society should not run interference for individuals. You do not sustain the virtues of individualism by actions on the part of government, the private sector, or the educational arena that undermine them." In the words of a recent TV commercial for a Wall Street firm: "We make money the old-fashioned way—we *earn* it!"

Great expectations were jolted, to indulge understatement, by the Great Depression. What most people today are unaware of is that the unprecedented, interventionist role of government the Great Depression required was initially viewed as temporary. Within a few short years that view changed dramatically as the economic system deteriorated and the New Deal programs took on the characteristics of a Band-Aid. It was not until this country began to gear up for what would become World War II that the Great Depression began to lift. By the time we entered the war an unarticulated change in the American worldview had already taken place; it was the responsibility of society (the public and private sectors) to be concerned with the social and economic welfare of individuals.

It is beyond the scope of this chapter to detail the diverse ways in which the war years reinforced both the change in individual expectations and society's responsibility for the individual. Those changes became crystal clear after World War II and they were encapsulated in what I term the "era of redefinition of self." That phrase refers to the fact that the post-World War II years are distinguished by the number of individuals and groups who explicitly and militantly proclaimed that they no longer would define themselves as society was accustomed to define and regard them. Blacks and other minorities, women, old people, handicapped people, gays, nurses, clinical psychologists, public school teachers—these are only some of the groups who in the process of redefining themselves sought to alter the relationships among their working, personal, and social lives. It was not, I must emphasize, a process riveting on one area of living. It was a far more radical process that essentially said: "I (we) have diverse needs and goals in work *and* living that have to be seen in relation to each other and to which society should make an accommodation."

On the day I wrote these words, President Reagan vetoed a trade bill containing the provision that a company with more than 100 employees must give 60 days' notice of its intention to close a plant. The bill was passed overwhelmingly in both houses of Congress, although it is uncertain whether there are enough votes in the Senate to override the veto. What is remarkable about this provision is what it reflects about altered conceptions of corporate responsibility for the welfare of individuals and their communities. A decade or more ago such a provision would have received the shortest of shrifts from a congressional committee. The point is that when we say "responsibility" we are giving expression to the value judgment that the arena of work phenomenologically and policywise cannot and should not be separated from other arenas of living.

I am describing what I consider to be a truly historical alteration in worldview about what one has a *right* to expect from daily living, an alteration we hardly comprehend in terms of its near- and long-term consequences. Perhaps the clearest example is the consequence of the women's liberation movement. For decades that movement centered around legal and moral issues. But as that movement stimulated remedial legislation, as its moral basis gained more widespread acceptance, new questions arose in regard to the arena of work. Was maternity leave a right? How long should such a leave be? For the sake of family cohesion and health, should there not also be paternity leave? And what about onsite day care?

In the April 1988 newsletter of the American Association of Retired People, several government-supported demonstration projects were reported involving IBM, the Remington Corporation, and the New York City Personnel Department. In each site a service has been developed for employees coping with elderly parents or other very ill family members. At IBM, for example, the service is essentially informational; at the Remington Corporation the service focuses on obtaining respite care. In all instances these services are justified in terms of self-interest, not altruism, as ways of maintaining employee efficiency. For me the important point is the recognition accorded to the porous, psychological boundaries between the work and personal-social arenas. But, it could be argued, it was always in the self-interest of corporations to do whatever needed to be done to keep employees efficient in their work. Why now? Why not 20 or 40 years ago? Changes in conception of self-interest are never independent of changes in worldview. And changes in worldview involve far more than changes in what is the "bottom line," that is, they are a response over time—usually vaguely articulated, if articulated at all—to altered realities that may appear to be unrelated but whose underlying relatedness does not become apparent or clear until later generations label the change. It is my opinion that we are into an era distinguished by a worldview the dynamics of which get their force from great expectations and the belief that society's major institutions have a responsibility to put flesh on the bones of those expectations.

Let me illustrate this by an example from the university. It used to be the case before World War II, and for a couple of decades after it, that when a department had an opening, it used customary informal channels to find the *man* they wanted. The phrase "old boys' network" was quite appropriate. But then came the women's liberation movement, and like *Ten Days That Shook the World*, the university had to adjust to a new reality. But that reality involved far more than the rights of women in the workplace of the university. If the university sought to accommodate that movement, it was because that movement was one of many such movements by groups pressuring for change. It was not the case that the university said that the role of women in the university should change, but that it was a long overdue righting of a wrong. Of course the university said that, but its spokespeople were quite aware that a redefinition of self was occurring in many other members of diverse groups in the society. They may not have been wildly enthusiastic about all these goings-on but they knew at some level that the ball game had changed. And it changed in several ways, the most important of which was a consequence of dual career marriages. If it was a man whom the department wanted, that man would ask questions about opportunities for his wife in the university or the community. This was also true if it was a woman being offered a university position. If both husband and wife sought faculty positions, the difficulty the university encountered increased dramatically. Any senior member of a university knows what I am talking about. Increasingly, the university can no longer select *an* individual for *a* position, period. Officially, of course, that is what the university does but phenomenologically it cannot proceed as if the personal life of a sought-after candidate is of secondary importance. It hires one person, but in actuality it hires two.

For several years now, my department at Yale has been unable to attract some people we wanted because we could not arrange for a spouse to be given an appointment in another department. This was such a frustrating problem that last year we requested the university to permit us to make offers to two outstanding psychologists who were married to each other. To our amazement, the university responded affirmatively. One instance does not a trend make, but it's an instance of how one particular workplace—the university—is being forced to change its accustomed view of the relationship between the personal and the professional.

Like meteorologists, we do a creditable job in predicting short-term consequences of the societal weather. In regard to long-term consequences our track record is far poorer. Much has been written in this century about the nature of work and the workplace. But in the early decades of this century, our theorists of industry assumed that there was nothing in the American worldview that would significantly alter what the workplace would or should be. Those who assumed otherwise were regarded as visionaries or radicals who did not understand America. But the visionaries and radicals proved to be far more correct than the professionals. The latter riveted on the workplace, the former looked more broadly on the social scene. It was not until after World War II that the professionals truly came to appreciate that the workplace is an interpersonal arena. Today that is a glimpse of the obvious, but why did it take so long for the obvious to be recognized? The answer, in brief, is that the world had changed and that change altered our view of the workplace. But that brings me to an important, and disheartening, impression: we are still riveted on the work site and largely ignoring ongoing changes in worldview that ineluctably will bring about a change in our view of the work site. Any conception of the work site that is not embedded in societal dynamics—their past, present and future—will turn out to be a relic of narrow thinking.

New Interdependencies Between Private Business and Public Education

I turn now to a set of issues that has received little thought and study by those interested in the workplace. These are issues that have a salience they never had before and will dramatically alter work sites. I refer to the relationship between our public schools and work sites. I have discussed this at some length in my book *Schooling in America: Scapegoat and Salvation* (Sarason, 1983). Let me summarize my argument:

1. Those who will write the history of this century will have to devote a long chapter to the unprecedented efforts of federal, state, and local bodies to improve educational outcomes by increased support of all kinds.

2. These efforts sought to change our schools in myriads of ways: their structure, relationship to the community, salaries, curricula, professional preparation of educators, and academic standards.

3. Most of these efforts have been failures. The result has been that the more things change, the more they remain the same: improvement in educational outcomes has been minimal; dropout rates are still scandalously high, especially in our urban centers; and some have argued that no dent at all has been made in scientific and cultural illiteracy.

4. Schools are uninteresting places for students and educational personnel. Albeit there are the usual exceptions, schools extinguish rather than reinforce the normal curiosity that children bring to school when they are enrolled.

5. All of the efforts to change and improve schools rest on an unarticulated axiom: Schooling should and best takes place in encapsulated classrooms in encapsulated schools. That axiom is invalid in whole or in part. As long as these efforts derive from or rest on that axiom, the sought-for improvement will not occur. This is a prediction I made 25 years ago and nothing has happened to disconfirm it.

So what universe of alternatives is available to us if we reject the axiom? Let me preface my answer by an anecdote I relate in my book. The education editor of the *New York Times* interviewed the Dean of Sciences for the City University of New York (CUNY) who began by reciting a familiar litany:

- more than a third of all who teach science in our schools have no credentials to do so;
- in the previous year the state of Connecticut had certified one teacher in mathematics, not atypical among the states;
- the teaching of science in high schools is very poor, and it is scandalously so in middle schools;
- there is no difference between public and private schools in these respects.

The editor then asked the dean what his university was doing to remedy the situation. He replied that each summer a number of black middle school students from the Bronx have the opportunity to work as assistants in labs to science faculty who are doing research. These students, on the average, are neither above nor below grade level. He went on to describe the transformation these youngsters undergo.

So what lesson did he draw from this for school? The answer was that this experience was what should be going on *inside* of schools. That, of course, is literally impossible. Instead of concluding that we look at our communities from the standpoint of the work sites they contain that could be used for educational purposes, he exposes his own adherence to the axiom that schooling should and best takes place in encapsulated classrooms in encapsulated schools.

So what alternatives are available to us? My answer is that we start looking imaginatively at work sites that will serve intellectual-educational purposes. In no way does my answer imply vocational training or goals. I'm not opposed to vocational education. I am opposed to schooling that: extinguishes curiosity, imparts abstractions devoid of personal significance, keeps apart life in and out of school, depends exclusively on memory for acquiring and retaining knowledge, makes for boredom, divides the world in two—the uninteresting world of school and the interesting world "out there." If we continue on the well travelled, traditional road of educational reform, we are doomed. The major obstacles to be overcome are not initially economic, political, or theoretical in the sense that we need better conceptions of how we go about changing what takes place within schools. The primary or initial problem is how we unimprison ourselves from a worldview about where schooling should best take place. It is a worldview that once confronted and challenged is both unsettling and liberating, and it is no wonder that we shrink from pursuing its implications for action. But that should occasion no surprise. Has there ever been a challenge to a worldview that was warmly embraced? Were challenges to the place of women and blacks in our worldview greeted with other than expressions of incredulity?

Let us look at this problem now from the standpoint of the work site. I offer the observation that as never before in our history, the industrial and corporate sectors are concerned with the inadequacies of our schools. These sectors have always had a vested interest in our schools, but in earlier decades of this century that interest was narrow and self-serving, that is, their concern was only from the standpoint of skill training appropriate to the workplace. That concern is still there and dominant, but it is now being altered by or suffused with anxiety deriving from the perception that our inadequate schools—especially our urban ones—threaten the social fabric. Do we already have an underclass, a kind of lumpenproletariat? Is it increasing? As a nation can we afford its economic, political, racial-ethnic implications? Can we tolerate an educational system the bulk of whose students seem to be cultural and scientific illiterates? What are the near and long-term consequences of the fact that the gulf between the haves and the have-nots in our society is widening?

I can sum up what I have gleaned from discussions with corporate leaders in this way: Something is wrong somewhere. Whatever we have done to beef up our educational system has hardly worked. The private sector is being negatively affected. What can we do to increase the motivation of students to stay in school and learn, to make them feel they will have a place in our society, a changing society that will require its citizens to be knowledgeable, skillful, and self-reliant? We are dependent on a good educational system as never before, and when we say "we," we refer to more than those of us with corporate responsibility.

How do we use work sites for intellectual and educational purposes, capitalizing on children's curiosity about what their world is and how it works? When I say "intellectual and educational purposes," I mean the broadening and deepening of children's knowledge of and skill with the substance of history, literature, science, and social studies. How do you make subject matter interesting and relevant in a child's experience? For example, there is a middle school on Long Island that has 600 students. In any one week three of them spend several hours in some community site as helpers, e.g., it may be a site devoted to day care, cerebral-palsied individuals, senior citizens, or some other handicapped or dependent group. The purpose of the program is not—except in a secondary way—geared to sensitizing students to the helping process. Associated with their supervised experience is a seminar, the purpose of which is to exploit the experience for what can be learned about biology, human development, history, and community organization.

This program was not undertaken lightly and the work sites were understandably hesitant about participating. Within a couple of years the sites sought more students and an increasing number of students sought to participate in this voluntary program. In fact, one year the students participated in writing and publishing a book about the program. These children, like those described earlier in the anecdote by the CUNY Dean of Sciences, were middle school children. The number of such programs are miniscule in number when compared to the number of schools in this country, but their conceptual and practical significance cannot be overestimated. Once you take seriously that work sites are possible and desirable places for intellectual and educational stimulation and growth because they are intrinsically interesting places to children in ways that schools are not and cannot be, you have taken the first step to meaningful educational reform. In *Schooling in America: Scapegoat and Salvation* (Sarason, 1983), I describe a conversation with the Dean of Arts and Sciences of the University of Hartford, who happened to be a physicist and a computer consultant to several insurance companies in that city. He agreed with my argument and then went on to ask: "What if we could use Aetna Life Insurance Company as an educational site? It boggles the mind when you realize that Aetna can be used to learn about mathematics, economics, health, meteorology, and God knows what else." This dean was one who each summer employed high school students to work on his and other people's research projects. Each summer his biggest kick comes from the knowledge that, unbeknownst to the students, they had learned calculus.

The changes I advocated between the worlds within and outside of schools are already taking place in the private sector. Let us contemplate an editorial in the journal *Science* by Abelson (1987):

Education and training within corporations of the United States is an important and growing industry. The dollars spent and the numbers of company students trained are comparable to the totals experienced by all the country's 4-year colleges and universities. A substantial portion of the training efforts of corporations is devoted to upgrading the capabilities of their blue-collar workers. The circumstances under which teaching is conducted vary from company to company, and at different locations in any given company. For the most part, the curricula are dictated by the company to serve company objectives, and the courses are conducted during working hours.

The United Auto Workers and Ford Motor Company have cooperated to create a novel and flexible UAW-Ford Employee Development and Training Program that merits close attention and possible replication elsewhere. In part this program represents recognition of the need for labor to be more literate and computer-knowledgeable if this nation is to compete in the future. The program is also responsive to deeply felt needs for self-improvement on the part of many of the employees. It focuses on the individual interests and goals of the worker, uses customized individual and group guidance materials, and provides networking and partnership of local educational and training organizations.

The two partners, labor and management, have sought the collaboration of the University of Michigan, which employs life-education advisers who have important roles in facilitating educational programs. The advisers are stationed at the various production plants and serve many functions, including friendly counseling. They help employees formulate and implement programs for self-improvement that are geared to the individual's talents and goals.

In the United States, Ford employs about 100,000 people who are represented by the UAW. They work at more than 70 locations where parts are made, subassemblies are produced, or vehicles are assembled. The previous educational attainments of the employees vary. About 25% have not completed high school. Another 60% stopped studies after completing high school. About 20% have had some college or university experience. Corresponding to this, a diversity of opportunities are available at each level. There are remedial programs for some. There is paid college tuition for others. More than 500 outside college-level institutions are involved. Nearly 100 of them conduct classes within the production plants. The union and the company jointly administer the program for which funds are available. An individual can obtain $2000 in tuition support annually to attend an accredited college or university. Attendance in classes is on the individual's time, not the company's. When training is required to meet specific job needs, the instruction is conducted during working hours. The fact that many employees are willing to spend their limited free time on classes and studies is impressive.

Many of the courses chosen by employees add to their literacy, communication skills, or mathematical competence. Courses on computers leading to and including programming are popular, as are courses in robotics. Some of the students choose subjects not directly related to their work, such as public speaking. (p. 875)

Abelson finds it impressive that "many employees are willing to spend their limited free time on classes and studies." What I would find remarkable is if they were unwilling to do so, and I would feel similarly if middle and high school students did not eat up opportunities that speak to their curiosity, interests, and sense of growth and competence.

If anything in the post-World War II era distinguishes efforts to understand and alter the workplace it is the aim to make that place interesting to those in it. And the same has been true in the myriads of efforts to make schools interesting places. In regard to the private sector, those efforts have not been all that productive, if only because the focus has been so narrow—that is, insensitive to the kinds of things Abelson finds so impressive. But compared to these efforts, those taken in regard to our schools have been miserable failures, to a degree that will continue to have adverse effects on the society.

I am not optimistic that the situation will change at the pace the national interest requires. My lack of optimism can be explained by quoting from Dewey (1900) who wrote:

> From the standpoint of the child, the great waste in the school comes from his inability to utilize the experiences he gets outside the school in any complete and free way within the school itself; while, on the other hand, he is unable to apply in daily life what he is learning in school. That is the isolation of the school—its isolation from life. When the child gets into the schoolroom he has to put out of his mind a large part of the ideas, interests, and activities that predominate in his home and neighborhood. So the school, being unable to utilize this everyday experience, sets painfully to work, on another tack and by a variety of means, to arouse in the child an interest in school studies. While I was visiting in the city of Moline a few years ago, the superintendent told me that they found many children every year who were surprised to learn that the Mississippi River in the textbook had anything to do with the stream of water flowing past their homes. The geography being simply a matter of the schoolroom, it is more or less of an awakening to many children to find that the whole thing is nothing but a more formal and definite statement of the facts which they see, feel, and touch every day. When we think that we all live on the earth, that we live in an atmosphere, that our lives are touched at every point by the influences of the soil, flora, and fauna, by considerations of light and heat, and then think of what the school study of geography has been, we have a typical idea of the gap existing between the everyday experiences of the child and the isolated material supplied in such large measure in the school. This is but an instance, and one upon which most of us may reflect long before we take the present artificiality of the school as other than a matter of course or necessity.
>
> Though there should be organic connection between the school and business life, it is not meant that the school is to prepare the child for any particular business, but that there should be a natural connection of the everyday life of the child with the business environment about him, and that it is the affair of the school to clarify and liberalize this connection, to

bring it to consciousness, not by introducing special studies, like commercial geography and arithmetic, but by keeping alive the ordinary bonds of relation. The subject of compound-business-partnership is probably not in many of the arithmetics nowadays, though it was there not a generation ago, for the makers of textbooks said that if they left out anything they could not sell their books. This compound-business-partnership originated as far back as the sixteenth century. The joint-stock company had not been invented, and as large commerce with the Indies and Americas grew up, it was necessary to have an accumulation of capital with which to handle it. One man said, "I will put in this amount of money for six months," and another, "So much for two years," and so on. Thus by joining together they got money enough to float their commercial enterprises. Naturally, then, "compound partnership" was taught in the schools. The joint-stock company was invented; compound partnership disappeared, but the problems relating to it stayed in the arithmetics for two hundred years. They were kept after they had ceased to have practical utility, for the sake of mental discipline—they were "such hard problems, you know." A great deal of what is now in the arithmetics under the head of percentage is of the same nature. Children of 12 and 13 years of age go through gain and loss calculations, and various forms of bank discount so complicated that the bankers long ago dispensed with them. And when it is pointed out that business is not done this way, we hear again of "mental discipline." And yet there are plenty of real connections between the experience of children and business conditions which need to be utilized and illuminated. The child should study his commercial arithmetic and geography, not as isolated things by themselves, but in their reference to his social environment. The youth needs to become acquainted with the bank as a factor in modern life with what it does, and how it does it; and then relevant arithmetical processes would have some meaning—quite in contradistinction to the time-absorbing and mind-killing examples in percentage, partial payments, etc., found in all our arithmetics. (pp. 75-78)

What John Dewey described in 1900 in *The School and Society* is no less true today, perhaps more true. The "great waste" goes on, the stakes are higher, and we are still imprisoned in a worldview that keeps apart arenas of experience unproductive for the individual, the school, the work site, and the society.

In this chapter, I have emphasized two themes. The first was that an attitudinal change has occurred that is making the boundaries between the work site and the personal-social arena of experience more porous. On the level of action or policy that change is small; on the level of individual expectations that change is profound, and we have hardly tried to understand its origins, strength, and implications for the future. The second theme was in two parts. The first concerns the efforts to improve our schools, to make them more interesting and challenging places for intellectual-educational growth. These efforts have failed, and will continue to fail. Second, unless those efforts seek to integrate schooling and work sites, both will be adversely affected.

It is obvious that I have successfully resisted the internal pressure to be, if not inspiring, at least optimistic and constructive in a practical sense. But the fact is that I am not optimistic that we can begin where we have to begin: by making a fundamental change in our usual conceptions of the nature of working and schooling. However, in pleading for that change, I regard myself as constructive, even though I know that reactions to what I advocate will vary from outright rejection at one extreme to tolerant amusement at the other. (The central point will be occupied by a few who will agree with me that something is radically wrong, albeit they will not find my ideas helpful.)

That the time you have spent reading this is not a total "small waste," I will end this chapter by telling a joke which encapsulates my feelings (but still is a good joke).

A journalist was assigned to the Jerusalem bureau of his newspaper. He got an apartment overlooking the Wailing Wall. After several weeks he became aware that, regardless of when he looked at the wall, he saw an old Jew praying vigorously. There must be a story here, the journalist concluded. So he went down, introduced himself, and asked the old, bearded Jew: "What are you praying for?" The old Jew replied: "What am I praying for? In the morning I pray for world peace. I go home, have a snack, and come back and pray for the eradication of illness and disease from the earth. Then I go home, have a glass of tea, and return to pray for the brotherhood of man."

The journalist was very much taken with the old Jew's sincerity and seriousness. He asked: "How long have you been praying for these wonderful things?" To which the old Jew replied: "How long? Twenty, maybe twenty-five years." The journalist could not believe his ears. "You mean, every day for all of these years you stand before this wall and pray for world peace, the eradication of illness and disease, and the brotherhood of man? How does it feel to pray for these things all of these years?" To which the old Jew replied: "How does it feel? It feels like talking to a wall."

References

Abelson, P. (1987). Editorial: Continuing education for blue-collar workers. *Science, 238,* p. 875.

Dewey, J. (1943). *The child and the curriculum, and the school and society.* Chicago: University of Chicago Press. (Original work published 1900)

Sarason, S. B. (1983). *Schooling in America: Scapegoat and salvation.* New York: Free Press.

PART III

Organizational Reactions to the New Competitiveness Forces and Their Impact on Workers

5 Achieving Competitiveness by Creating New Organization Cultures and Structures

EDWARD E. LAWLER III

It became obvious in the 1970s and moved center stage in the 1980s: American businesses are increasingly losing their competitive edge. In the 1960s Western Europe feared that American businesses would dominate the European economy and that Europeans would end up as poor consumers of American goods (see, e.g., Servan-Schreiber, 1968). Today, Americans worry that they will become poor consumers for Japanese goods (Grayson & O'Dell, 1988).

In just two decades, Europe has become a much stronger economic force and Asian countries, including Japan, Hong Kong, Taiwan, and Korea have had major successes in exporting goods to the United States. This has had a dramatic negative effect on the U.S. auto, steel, glass, rubber, and electronics industries. The list, of course, is longer than these major industries, but these industries are so visible and basic to any country's economy that when they begin to move offshore it is clear that a radical change has occurred in a country's industrial structure (Grayson & O'Dell, 1988). One can go on for pages citing the great amounts of data which indicate that many American businesses have lost their competitive advantage. But the focus of this chapter is not on proving the case; that has already been done. It is on what strategies organizations can take to recapture the advantage.

There is no question American industry is beginning to respond to foreign competition. Virtually every major U.S. corporation that is subject to foreign competition has made efforts to change its situation (see Lawler, Ledford, & Mohrman, 1989). Although many different things are being tried by American companies in order to improve their competitive position, three approaches appear to be dominant. The three approaches are very different in the actions they lead to and in their impact on organizational effectiveness and the quality of work life of individuals. This chapter will look at each of the three approaches and speculate about their long-term success as well as their implications for those of us who study organizations.

The first two of these approaches will be discussed only briefly because, on balance, they are the least interesting from an organizational research point of view. Most of the chapter will focus on the third approach because it has its clearest roots in the organizational behavior literature and has the most profound implications for research and the development of new management practices.

Although these three tracks or strategies will be treated as different and separate, I do not mean to imply that a single organization can't pursue all three of them simultaneously. Indeed, some large corporations are pursuing all three of them. In the case of most companies, however, one approach tends to dominate. The other strategies, if they are used at all, tend to be used in small parts of the organization, or in pieces that face different competitive situations. These strategies represent different understandings of why there are problems and different sets of assumptions as to how people in the United States can respond to the competitive problems. Thus, holding all three is, to a degree, internally inconsistent and not likely to occur.

A brief outline of each of the three strategies follows. The first strategy has as its dominant activity, doing the old better. In this approach little is done to change the basic way organizations are managed and deal with people. In manufacturing businesses it is often combined with heavy investment in new capital equipment in order to make the business more productive and to improve quality. This approach tends to emphasize traditional approaches to compensation, selection, and financial systems, but it emphasizes doing them better and paying a great deal more attention to the cost effectiveness of everything that is done in the organization, and in some cases a focus on quality. Often it leads to staff reductions and layoffs as well as corporate restructuring.

The second strategy involves a variety of approaches that have in common a high level of organization flexibility about how and where the organization obtains its products and operates its business. In essence, it accepts the international competitive situation as one where certain countries and certain locations have a natural advantage in producing certain products and in operating certain ways, and calls for the organization to align itself with these natural advantages. If for example, a product is labor intensive and therefore cheap labor is important, the company simply decides to manufacture its products in Mexico, Thailand, or wherever reliable cheap labor can be obtained. If some other organization has a tremendous competency to manufacture the product, then the organization doesn't try to manufacture at all; it simply becomes an importer. Often this type of organization ends up with worldwide operations and a number of strategic alliances in order to get its products manufactured and, in some cases, sold. Perhaps the best term for this second strategy is the *network organization* (Miles & Snow, 1986). Recently it has also been called the *value adding partnership* (Johnston & Lawrence, 1988). It clearly is an interesting approach, because it leads to a number of human resource management and organization design issues that are new and different from those in the traditional top-down bureaucratic corporation.

The third strategy involves the adoption of a new approach to the design and management of work. It has been called high performance management, high involvement management, high commitment management and participative management. This approach emphasizes getting individuals throughout the organization directly involved in managing the business in the expectation that this will lead to higher productivity and higher quality work (Lawler, 1986). This is the most interesting approach from an organizational behavior point of view because it calls for the redesign of a number of organizational systems and actually puts into practice many ideas which have been suggested by the organizational behavior literature for decades (e.g., McGregor, 1960).

The Competitive Problem

Four explanations are typically offered for the competitive problems of the United States. Those explanations are worth mentioning because they can drive the type of strategic response which organizations choose.

Perhaps the most common perception of why the U.S. has competitive problems is that the work force is overpaid and undermotivated. Survey data suggest that this is the perception generally held by management. It is usually buttressed by the argument that unions have ruined the productivity of many manufacturing locations because they have bargained for restrictive work rules and high wages. It is also supported by data which show the relatively high cost of American labor compared to labor elsewhere and by data which show that the skills of the American work force are lower than those in Japan and other countries (Grayson & O'Dell, 1988).

The second reason given is that the American business environment is not a favorable one for businesses. This point stresses the amount and type of government regulation that exists and the investment situation in the United States, including relatively high interest rates.

The third argument focuses on the skills and motivation of American managers. This explanation is commonly put forward by union leaders and some academics. It argues that American managers are overpaid, undermotivated and generally not as competent as their foreign counterparts. This argument gains its credibility from the extraordinarily high wages of American executives and the fact that many Japanese companies have come to the United States and been quite successful in businesses where U.S. managers have done poorly. For example, increasingly Japanese auto and consumer electronics companies are successfully manufacturing in the United States using large numbers of Japanese managers and American workers (MacDuffie, 1988).

The fourth explanation points to the general management style that exists in the United States. American companies mastered the top-down bureaucratic control approach to management in the 1950s and 1960s and have stuck to it with great tenacity. It can be argued, however, that it has been outdated by numerous changes which have taken place in society, the work force, the world economy and the demands of modern technology (see, e.g., Peters, 1987).

There undoubtedly is some truth in all four of these explanations. Before we consider them further, however, we need to look at each of the three strategies in more depth. When we return to them it needs to be in the context of what strategy or strategies can help make U.S. companies more effective.

Strategy I: Doing the Old Better

The most frequently adopted strategy for gaining an international competitive advantage is doing the old better (Lawler, Ledford, & Mohrman, 1989). It in effect assumes the major problem in the United

States is that the work force is not motivated and that organizations have gotten "fat and flabby." The popular press is regularly filled with stories in which companies talk about the importance of doing a better job of paying for performance (usually individual performance), paying more attention to quality, and of course reducing overhead—the inevitable focus of cost reduction efforts. Organization after organization in the manufacturing arena has done an assessment of its operating cost and found that it is a "bloated" bureaucracy with too many levels of management, too much staff support, and in general too much overhead. The typical response is to cut out massive numbers of employees and to put extreme pressure on people throughout the organization to work harder or be laid off or dismissed. Redundant managers are typically offered early retirement or severance packages and, as a result, the ranks of management have shrunk significantly in companies such as General Electric and Kodak.

If there is a union present in the organization, the organization typically goes into a concession-bargaining mode in which it demands significant givebacks in wages, benefits, and work rules. If there is no union, then the organization simply emphasizes rationalizing its work force and ends up dramatically reducing the number of employees it has and its total cost of doing business. Typically, this approach does not question the fundamental hierarchical nature of the organization and the fact that control rests at the top levels. Indeed, if anything, it reinforces these views by the way the cost reductions are handled.

A complete list of organizations that have taken this approach would read much like the Fortune 500 list of industrials. Just to mention one example, the breakup at AT&T led to not just AT&T going through this exercise, but to a number of the newly independent baby Bells doing it as well. For example, Pacific Bell has reduced its work force by over 30,000 employees. General Motors provides another example of an organization which has reduced its management overhead and the number of its management layers. Even IBM, often cited as the most admired U.S. corporation, has gone through this exercise and has ended up with a significantly smaller work force.

There is no question that when organizations adopt the strategy of doing the old better, they can make themselves more competitive. In many cases, older organizations have indeed become bloated and can stand some reduction in their overall cost structure. There also is no question that they can do many of the basics better. For example, few organizations that are traditionally managed do a great job of selecting new employees, appraising performance, paying for performance, training individuals, focusing on quality, and so on. The fact that international competition has put pressure on them to improve in these areas is neither surprising nor particularly revolutionary. It has, however, allowed organizational researchers to do further development work in many of the traditional areas of personnel psychology. It also has led to extensive work in areas concerned with outplacement, mergers and acquisitions, and careers.

Strategy I has led to dramatic changes in the case of some large conglomerates. Recently, companies like ITT, Westinghouse, and General Electric, which have operated in many businesses, have moved to simplify their organization by reducing the number of businesses in which they operate. An important part of the motivation for this seems to have been a decision by top management to gain more effective control over these organizations. As Peters (1987) and others have pointed out, in many diverse organizations top management adds little value and cannot control the organization very effectively. One way of improving the organization is to reduce diversity and create an organization which is more manageable in a top-down manner.

Strategy I can also be aided by moving certain operations to new locations where they run more successfully and can practice traditional top-down management more easily. A number of companies—General Motors and Rockwell, for example—have moved some of their manufacturing operations to nonunion areas of the U.S. or to Mexico, where the combination of cheap labor and geographic proximity make it a very attractive manufacturing location. Cheap labor is particularly important for top-down managed organizations because it makes it economically viable to use people to do routine repetitive work.

Parallel Participation Process

In many organizations, doing the old better also includes doing one thing that is new. A number of manufacturing companies have adopted "quality programs" (e.g., Quality Circles and, in union settings, Quality of Worklife programs) that involve a limited form of employee participation. These programs have also been used in some service industries, but a good guess is that they are much more prevalent in manufacturing companies (Lawler & Mohrman, 1985).

Total quality programs include more than just participative problem solving activities, but from an organizational behavior point of view probably their most interesting feature is their use of quality circles and other forms of special problem-solving and participation groups. Typically these are combined with quality measurement programs and an extensive communication and training program. The training typically involves teaching a number of people in the organization statistical process control, problem analysis and problem-solving skills, and sometimes group participation skills.

There is a growing body of research and theory that addresses the effectiveness of Quality Circles and other problem-solving participative processes (Lawler, 1986; Ledford, Lawler, & Mohrman, 1988). It is generally agreed that they are best thought of as parallel participation processes. They are parallel because they do not change the traditional hierarchical operation of the organization; instead, they create a special organization that operates in a new and different way. This parallel or quality circle organization has different leadership, norms, and structures, and requires different skills. It is beyond the scope of this chapter to go into a detailed analysis of the effectiveness of this type of participation. It is worth noting, however, that parallel participation structures can produce meaningful results. Employees typically are eager to become involved and when they are involved, they gain valuable skills and offer valuable suggestions to the organization. Thus, there is no question that they can help a traditional organization that is trying to improve its way of operating.

The problem with these programs is that they are programs and as such tend to be seen as temporary activities. Because of this and a number of other features, they typically do not become institutionalized nor do they lead to a new form of organization. To a degree they represent a quick and often temporary fix that can help improve an organization's competitive standing but does not change the fundamental way that an organization operates. Thus, they run quickly into the very organizational pathologies which led to their creation. They feed their ideas back into the existing organization, and that organization is expected to process them. Unfortunately, the ideas often get lost in the bureaucracy and meet resistance because managers in the middle of the organization are threatened by them and resent the fact that they were not involved in the process themselves. In addition, the ideas are often inappropriate because the employees do not have enough information and knowledge about the overall operation of the business. From their point of view the ideas are excellent, but they don't know about the overall organization strategy or many of the environmental constraints which exist; as a result they often come up with ideas which are impractical or outdated.

Finally, parallel participation structures are expensive to run in their own right and, as a result, may ultimately be challenged from a cost-benefit perspective. Training individuals who participate is expensive, but what ultimately can become even more expensive is the amount of meeting time that these programs take. This is resented by managers who lose their subordinates' production while they are in problem-solving groups. Typically, there is no reward for the manager who supports and encourages the groups, only punishment if their production falls because their subordinates are losing production time to participate.

In summary, parallel participation processes often can help a traditional organization improve its operating effectiveness. They give individuals additional skills, and they can make individuals potentially much more valuable to the organization. If they are combined with a serious total quality program such as those advocated by Deming, Juran, Conway, and Crosby, they can also sharpen up the measurement systems in an organization, cut some of the costs that are associated with poor quality, and focus employees on the fundamental management approach of the organization. The one qualification that seems to be appropriate here concerns the adoption by some companies of a total quality orientation, which does seem to be leading to some fundamental change and might ultimately represent a fourth strategy. This already seems to be the case for the U.S. plants of Japanese companies such as Honda, Toyota, and Sony.

Technology

Many manufacturing organizations that have adopted Strategy I have combined it with the introduction of new manufacturing technology. Highly automated manufacturing equipment is often installed, and in the most advanced companies computer-integrated manufacturing systems and paperless factories have been created (Zubhoff, 1988). In many respects, the use of this technology seems to represent the ultimate way to reduce labor costs and to create an environment that is highly controllable by management, or at least this seems to be the hope of some companies which install it. Increasingly, evidence is appearing that traditionally managed companies that install modern information and manufacturing technology end up with significant problems. These problems tend to come about because of the misfit between the management style and the technology which is adopted (Zubhoff, 1988). Much of the early writing on information technology assumed that it was either neutral with respect to management style or that it could be used most effectively in the service of a traditional top-down management style.

The argument that information technology favors traditional top-down management is based on the assumption that it makes possible a kind of close control which cannot be exercised in a manual environment. It makes it possible because tremendous amounts of information can be gathered, processed, and used for control purposes. The data, however, from environments where automated equipment and information technology have been installed, suggest that they may be incompatible with traditional top-down management styles (Majchrzak, 1988; Zubhoff, 1988). One reason for this has to do with the ability of traditional supervision to be effective in an automated environment. In a traditional manufacturing environment, supervisors can often look at individuals and easily tell whether they are performing their work effectively. In a highly automated environment this simply is not possible. Often employees are doing work that supervisors do not understand and quick observation cannot reveal whether they are doing the job effectively, ineffectively, or for that matter, at all.

In addition, the kind of employees that end up working in automated and information technology environments often resist traditional top-down control. They gain a sense of empowerment from the skills that they develop; as a result, ordering them to do something, telling them certain information is not available to them, etc., simply does not fit with their view of how they should be managed.

Finally, particularly in those situations where information technology is available, employees often end up with access to information and skills that previously were restricted to management. Thus, employees tend to expect a different relationship with the organization and to be involved in more decision making.

In short, the argument is that automation and information technology are not neutral with respect to management style. To be utilized effectively, they need to be combined with more participative management styles. Therefore, they often are not the best way for traditionally managed firms to improve their economic performance. Indeed, they may worsen the economic performance of traditionally managed companies because installing them represents a large cost; if they are not utilized in an effective way, the cost cannot be recovered.

Likely Gains

There are no good data on just how much improvement an organization can expect from a strong and effective program that emphasizes doing the old better. A guess is that it often can lead to a 15-20% improvement in operating performance and that in some cases this can be enough to significantly help an organization's international competitive position. This number is arrived at based largely upon the amount of cost-reduction organizations seem to be able to accomplish when they have focused on reducing management overhead and unnecessary operating costs. Of course, this is just an overall number. It can be much larger in organizations that start from a low base or a poor performance history. Those organizations that have truly become bloated bureaucracies with poor internal management systems clearly can gain much more than 15-20%, while an organization like IBM, which has done a good job of managing for decades, probably has much less to gain from this type of change strategy.

While Strategy I typically leads to improvements in operating results, there is a real question whether it leads to improvements in the quality of work life for individuals in the organization. Indeed, it is likely that rather than leading to an increase, it may lead to a decrease. Basically, it does little to change the fundamental work situation of most individuals in the organization. Since it retains the hierarchical bureaucratic model, most jobs in the organization end up being repetitive, unenriched jobs; and most individuals end up with relatively low power, few opportunities for personal growth and development, and little control over their personal destiny.

In many respects, the work situation of individuals may get worse with the adoption of this strategy. Insecurity and threat are created by the inevitable reductions in jobs and people. In many traditional organizations such as IBM and AT&T, one of the great sources of satisfaction for individuals was the job security guarantee which these organizations offered. Although the challenge level may have been low in many jobs, the threat level and stress level were also low. In a world where suddenly 10%, 15%, or 20% of the employees are let go by the organization, the stress level has to be much higher. The stress can be compounded if new technology is tried and employees are suddenly asked to operate new high technology equipment.

Finally, in many organizations the effect of Strategy I is to take some of the slack out of the organization. This can have the effect of reducing some of the prerequisites associated with being in a successful, traditionally managed organization. These prerequisites include the chance to socialize and go to training activities, meetings, and other events that remove individuals from their day-to-day work activities. When an organization is going though a Strategy I approach to improving effectiveness, many of these prerequisites and benefits disappear because cost controls on travel, training, and so forth are put into place. Finally, career tracks are disrupted and promotions become less likely because the hierarchical positions simply are not there any more.

In short, although there is relatively little evidence on the impact of Strategy I on quality of work life, there is good reason to believe that it is largely negative, even for those who survive the downsizings which are so prevalent. This in turn may lead to lower commitment on the part of individuals because their traditional psychological contract with the organization has been broken. The organization is no longer the secure, lifetime employer that it was. This in turn can lead to individuals looking elsewhere for employment and considering career changes even if they personally have not lost out as a result of the strategy.

Finally, there is the issue of how long-term the savings realized from Strategy I are. Cynics point out that large bureaucratic organizations go through spasms of cutting costs and that the current activities may be just another round of these. Large staff groups and many layers of management occur because of the inherent needs of traditional organizations for control and good top-down decisions. Thus, it is hardly surprising that over time they tend to add people who are assigned to control-oriented positions. This argument suggests that not only will the Strategy I approach tend to produce limited gains; these gains may also be temporary.

Strategy II: Competitive Repositioning and Networking

The essence of Strategy II is for an organization to locate its various operations and functions wherever and with whomever there is a competitive advantage. This location can be onshore or offshore; indeed it can be in another company such that the organization ends up with suppliers that do all or part of its manufacturing, engineering and marketing. It is perhaps easiest to see how this strategy unfolds with a manufacturing organization. Increasingly, manufacturing organizations can position their production facilities anywhere in the world to take advantage of the availability of labor, low labor costs, raw material supplies, and favorable government regulations because with modern transportation and communications technology, products can be in the United States ready for sale in a few hours or, at most, days.

Strategic positioning doesn't have to involve only doing manufacturing elsewhere in the world. Engineering can be done in a number of locations around the world. For example, currently companies are doing microelectronics engineering in Israel because there is a ready supply of electronics engineers there. Similarly, Taiwan and Scotland have a good supply of engineers, so they can be used as a location for engineering centers. Carrying strategic positioning one step further, organizations can decide that they don't need to do manufacturing at all. They can simply subcontract to someone who is particularly good at it and has a favorable manufacturing situation. The U.S.based organization may end up as a designer and marketer of products rather than as a manufacturer. Several years ago *Business Week* magazine referred to this strategy rather derisively as the "Hollow Corporation" model.

There are a number of organizations that are using the strategic positioning or networking strategy. Nike, and other U.S. shoe companies are a classic example. They do nothing but design and market their products. They use manufacturers in Asia to do all of their manufacturing. This gives them relatively low manufacturing costs and the ability to rapidly change the styles and production levels. They, in essence, have no ongoing responsibility for their manufacturing work force and don't have to worry about things like severance pay, U.S. benefit levels and environmental protection, safety, and so forth, nor do they have to worry about how their manufacturing employees are managed.

Often, the strategic positioning strategy leads organizations to an alliance or network model. In the alliance model organizations form relationships with other organizations to fill in the pieces of their product line or to perform functions that they can't perform effectively (Miles & Snow, 1986). This model is increasingly prevalent in the auto industry. Ford, for example, owns a part of Mazda, a Japanese car manufacturer, and sells Mazda-made cars—some of which are made in the U.S.—through its Ford dealerships. Of course, when they are sold in the Ford dealerships they have the Ford name on them and are sold as Ford products. The reality, however, is that Ford has decided that there is a part of the auto market in which they cannot compete, given their costs and capabilities, and they have decided to fill that part of their product line with a Mazda car, which is designed in the U.S. and Japan but manufactured in the United States.

Similarly, General Motors has turned over their factory in Fremont, California, to Toyota to manage. Toyota, in turn, manufactures a car there that is sold through both General Motors and Toyota dealers. This alliance came about because General Motors found itself unable to successfully manage the Fremont plant; and Toyota, because of its growing sales, needed a U.S. manufacturing base.

In the world of computers, a great deal of strategic positioning has taken place over the last few years. For example, AT&T has put its name on and sold Italian made Olivetti computers in the United States while Olivetti has sold AT&T computers in Europe. This came about because AT&T had little capability to manufacture low-cost personal computers. Its U.S. manufacturing operations clearly were too high-cost to be viable in the highly price-competitive personal computer business, so they bought part of Olivetti and had it manufacture a personal computer in Italy that was designed in California.

As Johnston and Lawrence (1988) point out, McKesson, a multibillion dollar health care company, has successfully used a network strategy to put itself at the hub of a large business. Most motion pictures are produced by network organizations, as the old studios that did everything have given way to networks of organizations that do different parts of the production and marketing process. Finally, and somewhat ironically, faced with high wages in Japan the Japanese electronics company Uniden does no manufacturing in Japan; it only does engineering and marketing there.

Effectiveness of Strategic Positioning Strategy

There is no question that the strategic positioning model has worked well for many organizations. Companies like Nike, Reebok, and Benneton have used it effectively in the consumer products market. Other companies have used it to reposition their manufacturing capabilities by moving their manufacturing to low wage locations. Indeed, it may be the only way for American companies to be competitive in businesses which are highly labor intensive. It also fits businesses which are very dynamic because it minimizes the commitments of an organization to employees, plant, and equipment. It clearly is a strategy which will continue to proliferate and succeed.

Little is known about the effects of the strategic positioning strategy on quality of work life. Overall, it may be more positive than negative. Particularly if it moves repetitive work out of the United States into cultures where it is a better fit with the values and aspirations of the people, it can have an overall positive effect. The problem, of course, is that it may reduce total employment in the United States and lead to greater job insecurity and, ultimately, unemployment.

One hope is that it can keep in the United States the higher value-added, more complex knowledge work that will provide interesting jobs for the U.S. work force. One trend, however, suggests the potential reversal of the traditional pattern of "good work" staying in the United States and low challenge jobs being done overseas. The Japanese auto companies are increasingly manufacturing in the United States, but doing their engineering and design work in Japan. A similar trend is developing in the electronics area with respect to T.V. sets. Carried to an extreme, the United States could end up as a major manufacturing location for Japanese designed products. The overall impact of this on the quality of work life in the United States certainly would be negative because of the type of work which would move out of the country.

It is difficult to assess the impact of network organizations on employment stability. It would seem that those organizations that are at the hub of the network could provide relatively stable employment, since they can easily adjust to change by realigning the network rather than by restructuring themselves; indeed, this is the major advantage of this strategy. The fate of the organizations and employees that are not central to the network is less clear. They could end up in very insecure positions as they apparently often do in the Japanese auto industry (Johnston & Lawrence, 1988). However, if they are very skillful at joining new networks, they too could be rather stable. For example, shoe manufacturers could shift from making Nike shoes to making Reebok shoes if that is what is popular.

Among the most interesting issues that come out of the strategic positioning approach are those having to do with human resource management systems. Very little is known about how to design and operate human resource management systems in organizations which are highly networked and based on alliances and temporary relationships. There are a great number of unknowns and challenges in managing the traditional multinational organization. Pay structures, career development, movement of foreign nationals, etc., all pose interesting challenges to such corporations. These are compounded greatly, however, when the issue is one of managing an organization that depends on its alliances with other corporations, many of which are foreign based.

It seems clear that negotiating skills are very important in any organization which is based on alliances. Thus, career tracks and training programs need to focus on how negotiating skills can be developed and on developing individuals who can influence decisions through methods other than traditional hierarchical power. In essence, in this kind of organization, the traditional hierarchy is in many respects obsolete. However, unlike the high involvement organizations that will be considered next, power doesn't necessarily move because of efforts to see that decisions are made at lower levels. Rather, it moves because it rests with individuals who do the strategic alliance building and win-win marketing.

The networking model in particular leads to interesting issues concerning reward systems. For example, performance appraisal no longer easily fits into the traditional one-over-one supervisory model. When individuals are working in a network-type organization, there are often multiple individuals who see their performance and are critical to their evaluation. Thus it seems that performance appraisal models need to be based on multiple inputs and in some cases inputs from individuals who are not employees of the organization. In addition, pay grades which are based on number of subordinates don't make any sense because individuals can have extremely demanding and complex jobs even though they supervise no one.

The kind of career tracks that individuals need in order to be managers in the network type of organization may need to be different than in the traditional hierarchical organization. For example, much of what is done in the networking organization at the managerial level has to involve linking and integrating activities. Preparation for this in many cases may require careers that involve working in other organizations and certainly in multiple functions. Thus organizations may need to work out career tracks that involve loaning employees to other organizations, perhaps their business partners, and rewards for individuals who take these positions.

In summary, the argument has been made that particularly in the human resource management area, moving to a networking approach calls for very different human resource management practices and approaches. Unlike Strategy I, which simply calls for traditional well-developed models of pay, selection, career development, and so forth, repositioning and networking require the development of new thinking and new approaches. If, as seems likely, organizations in the United States are increasingly going to adopt the strategic positioning approach, there should be many research opportunities for individuals interested in developing new and innovative approaches to human resources management.

From an organizational design point of view there also should be a number of interesting research topics that develop out of the adoption of the network approach. Just as new human resource management approaches are needed with the adoption of this approach, new approaches to organization design and structure clearly are in order. Particularly because of the different power relationship that exists between partners in a network-type organization, the use of traditional organization designs is not likely to be effective. In many ways, these organizations are like matrix organizations because they rely upon multiple reporting relationships and carefully balanced priorities (Davis & Lawrence, 1977; Galbraith, 1977). The problem is that many U.S. organizations tried and failed to successfully implement matrix organization approaches. At least one argument is that they failed not because matrix organizations are inherently flawed, but because the implementation was poorly done and lacked a good knowledge base. This suggests that with the growth of networking organizations a great deal more research is called for on how to manage and structure organizations that align themselves in nontraditional ways.

Overall, strategic positioning through network organizations and other new forms of organization represents an interesting and potentially powerful strategy for an American organization to use. It also represents an interesting strategy for researchers in the field of human resource management and organization design. Potentially, it can lead to new forms of organization that require very different human resource management practices. The research opportunities are likely to be great. As far as employees are concerned it can also be a relatively positive move. Strategic positioning may create more opportunities for individuals to function in work situations where they have meaningful work and the opportunity to develop new and different skills. Like matrix organizations, network organizations probably are not the place for individuals who have low tolerance for ambiguity and need clear-cut status relationships in order to be satisfied, but for many others they may be a good fit.

Strategy III: High Involvement Organizations

The third strategy that has emerged is the most interesting from an organizational behavior point of view. In many ways it represents an evolution of thinking which began in the organizational psychology literature of the 1940s and 1950s. At that time writers such as Lewin, McGregor, Argyris, and Likert stressed the desirability of organizations being managed in a more participative and democratic manner. This led to a long series of studies showing the advantages and disadvantages of democratic leadership styles. Interestingly, these studies were done in traditional organizations that by and large were managed in a hierarchical manner. This is an important point because, as we will see later, one argument is that participation and employee involvement only make sense when done in a congruent work setting.

Some of the earlier writing also focused on issues of work design, pay systems, and indeed did argue changes not just in leadership style but in other features of the organization's design. Theory Y, as expounded by McGregor (1960), put into a few simple statements the values of participative management.

The problem with the early writings on participative management was that although some people read them, few organizations adopted the practices suggested by them. There are a number of reasons for this including the fact that in many cases the authors were not presenting a full-blown organizational model that could be adopted. In many cases, they were simply arguing for new leadership or communication practices. But perhaps more fundamental was the fact that there was little reason to change. Reports did show that the traditional top-down structures produced relatively low levels of job satisfaction and even damaged individuals' mental and physical health (Work in America, 1973); nevertheless, U.S. organizations were highly profitable and most corporations felt little need to change their traditional management style.

As noted earlier, the dominance of American management and American organizations began to disappear in the 1970s, and as a result some organizations began to take a much more serious look at the whole idea of participative management (Lawler, 1986). This undoubtedly was further spurred by the success of companies like Volvo with their team approach to building cars, and of course the perception, whether accurate or not, that the Japanese used a more participative management style. In any case, during the 1970s and 1980s some large U.S. corporations looked seriously at the idea of a more employee involvement-oriented approach to management and decided that it was the right management style for them. Companies like Motorola, TRW and Xerox stated highly participative philosophies of management and have gone about implementing them throughout their organizations.

A number of organizations have instituted employee involvement in parts of their company. For example, Procter & Gamble has converted almost all of its manufacturing organization to what they call high performance or technician work systems. Virtually every major manufacturing company in the United States has one or more plants that have a gain-sharing plan or a high performance work system (Lawler, 1986; Lawler, Ledford, & Mohrman, 1989). Thus in a relatively short period of time, there has been a significant adoption of participative management practices by a number of U.S. corporations.

As a result of the increasing rate of adoption and the research which has been done on participatively managed organizations, it is now possible to outline in considerable detail how a high involvement organization should be designed. Less can be said about how effective they are, because in most cases the data simply aren't available. But before discussing the data on economic effectiveness and quality of work life, we need to look at the actual characteristics of a high involvement organization.

Characteristics of High Involvement Organizations

Descriptions of organizations typically start out by pointing out that all organizations are made up of multiple systems. Increasingly, in the last 20 years theories have gone on to stress that effectiveness is a product of the congruence among the different systems. It is not, for example, good enough to have a well-administered reward system if in fact the reward system does not fit the structure of the work, the information system, and so forth. Little data exist to support the congruence argument, but it has an inherent logic to it which seems to have led to its widespread acceptance in the organization theory literature (see, e.g., Galbraith, 1977; Nadler & Tushman, 1988).

Although congruence is argued for, it is rarely specified what, in fact, constitutes congruence among the different organizational systems.

Issues like what type of information system fits enriched jobs and what type of leadership behavior fits a decentralized organization are often discussed. But there is little specification of what a totally congruent overall set of organizational practices are, and few tests are specified for determining congruence or fit.

In addition to the problems of determining what constitutes congruence, most views of organization design identify different key features of an organization. Models range all the way from those that talk about only 3 or 4 systems in an organization to those that specify 7 to 10. This problem, however, is not always serious; in many cases the theories that identify fewer systems typically have incorporated some of the systems from the more detailed approaches into the limited categories in their approach. For example, some organizations talk about human resource management systems while others talk about separate systems for selection, training, and rewarding individuals. In discussing what a congruent high involvement organization looks like, eight features of the organization will be explored so as to be relatively complete in specifying what constitutes a high involvement organization.

The overall organization principle which is central to the high involvement organization model is that information, power, knowledge and rewards should be located at the lowest practical organizational level. This is in contrast to traditional approaches which argue for power, information, knowledge and rewards to be located at the top of an organization. Both the traditional and the high involvement model argue for congruence in the sense that they advocate the locating of all four of these factors together in an organization. The high involvement model argues that they should be located in the hands of the individual performing the work or delivering the service, while the traditional model argues that they should be located in the hands of senior management so that senior management can coordinate, direct, and motivate the work of others.

It is one thing to specify that in the high involvement model information, knowledge, power, and rewards need to be pushed down to the lowest level; it is another to come up with practical, organizational systems which in fact accomplish this. It is precisely in this area where significant progress has been made in the last ten years. As the practices which are characteristic of high involvement organizations are reviewed, it should become apparent that quite a bit of technology development has occurred so that in many cases it is now practical to talk

TABLE 5.1 Organization and Work Design

Themes	Practices
Involvement in business	Teams or enriched jobs
Ownership over product, service, and customer	Flat, lean structure
Felt responsibility	Product, service or customer based Task forces, diagonal slice policy groups Employee membership on boards

about individual performers having a significant say in how their work is done, having them understand the functioning of the organization, having them be rewarded based on organizational effectiveness, and finally, having them be quite knowledgeable about the overall operation of the business.

Organization and Work Design

The literature on organization and work design gives a rather clear picture of what an organization needs to look like if it is going to be consistent with an involvement strategy (Hackman & Oldham, 1980). Table 5.1 summarizes this literature in terms of themes and actual organization design practices. As can be seen from the table, it argues that in order to foster involvement in the operation of the organization, jobs and the overall structure of the organization need to deviate from the traditional hierarchical approach. Through teams or job enrichment, individuals should have considerable say over how their particular work is done and how their work areas operate. Through flattening the organization structure, organization levels that are chiefly responsible for control and direction need to be eliminated

The overall organization structure needs to focus more on products, services, and customers than on functions. This is crucial to giving individuals an opportunity to receive feedback and to making them accountable for the effectiveness of their performance. Finally, in order to allow individuals to participate in larger strategy issues and policy development, the use of task forces and policy groups is called for.

Taken together these organization and job design practices should locate a great deal of decision-making power, information, and knowl-

TABLE 5.2 Physical Layout Design

Themes	Practices
Egalitarian	Equal access to parking, dining, entrances
Support work design	Similar offices
	Laid out around team structure
Facilitate communication	Meeting areas, few walls

edge in the hands of the work performer. By themselves none of these practices are new or unproven as far as the organization theory and job design research literature is concerned. Perhaps the most nontraditional practice is the use of task forces and diagonal-slice policy groups to make major organizational strategy and design decisions. An extension of this is the idea of putting employee representatives on the board of directors. Task forces and employee board members are not present in most organizations, even in those that may have gone to flat structures and team-based job designs. They are included here, however, because they are a logical extension of individuals participating in important decisions that affect their work lives. Without them, employees can end up simply executing tasks and having little or no say in the overall strategy, direction, and operation of their organization.

Physical Layout and Design

Closely related to the issue of organization and work design is the physical layout of the organization. Virtually everyone is familiar with the typical physical layout in a hierarchical, top-down organization. Careful gradations of status symbols exist and they are allocated on the basis of hierarchical position. This clearly reinforces an internal culture of power resting at the top of the organization and the idea of power being vested in positions rather than in individuals. It also strongly encourages individuals who want status symbols to orient their career toward moving upward.

As Table 5.2 shows, the key to a high involvement organization is a physical layout that minimizes status differences. The argument in favor of an egalitarian physical layout stems very much from the view that in a high involvement organization power should move around the orga-

TABLE 5.3 Information System

Themes	Practices
Open	Distributed technology/on line capability/user friendly
Two way	Regular financial reviews
Local ownership	Suggestion processing system
Performance oriented	Attitude surveys
Human system data	Performance feedback against goals

nization to those individuals who have the knowledge and informatio to exercise it. It should not simply move to the highest level. Such thing as egalitarian prerequisites and facilities are a symbolic as well a practical way to encourage individuals to treat each other based on wha they have to contribute to a decision rather than on what their particula position is.

The physical layout also should support the job design structure particularly if teams are used. It can do this by encouraging face-to-fac interaction and providing teams with a physical environment that al lows them to meet, solve problems, and gather the information that the need. It also can lead to the kind of informal social contact tha facilitates socialization and builds group cohesiveness.

Information Systems

The information system is critical to the success of any organization Traditional systems are oriented toward providing information abou performance upward and directions downward. As shown in Table 5.3 in a high involvement organization the orientation is very different. Th key is to structure the information system such that it provides a fre flow of information, so that people in performer roles have a good sens of the organization's direction and performance. It also needs to provid individuals in higher level roles with data about the condition of th human system of the organization and about how effectively the orga nization is operating from a decision-making, information-processing and cultural point of view.

In many cases the key to developing an information system consistent with high involvement management is the use of new forms of information technology. Computer networking creates the possibility for much greater amounts of information to be delivered to any performer. It also makes it possible for performers to handle much of the necessary coordination and information exchange without the use of a hierarchy and a supervisor to link different pieces or parts of the organization together. Thus it is an important piece of technology in making possible a more involvement-oriented management style in large, complex manufacturing operations and in many multilocation and large-location organizations. It, of course, is not enough by itself; the organization also needs to be sure that it has ways of processing suggestions, providing employees with good data about how the organization is functioning, and developing informal communication links. Much of this needs to be done on a face-to-face basis so individuals can ask questions and become comfortable with interpreting business information; thus it calls for a number of meetings.

Managerial Role

The traditional managerial role in an organization involves controlling, directing, and priority setting. In a more participative environment very different behaviors are required of managers. As is shown in Table 5.4, managers need to be in more of a leadership role and engage in a number of practices that empower people and lead to their being involved in the management of the business and their own jobs. They also need to place a great deal of emphasis on monitoring the effectiveness of the organization and the external environment. They, more than anyone else, are in a position to sense changes in the environment and help position the organization effectively from a competitive point of view.

Perhaps the hardest part of the managerial role in a high involvement organization is the monitoring of the decision processes and operation of the organization. It is hard because the manager needs to walk a very fine line between abdication and overcontrol. It is not all right for a manager to stand back and say, "The group decided and, therefore, there is nothing I can do even though I disagree with the decision and think the decision was poorly made." Similarly, it is wrong for the manager to preemptively reject group suggestions and ideas about how things

TABLE 5.4 Manager's Role

Themes	Practices
Leadership	Monitor culture
Visionary	Do–don't watch
Empowering	Manage symbols
Enabling	Share power and information
Participative	Set goals
	Model good decision-making process
	Develop values/philosophy statement and use it
	Benchmark performance
	Monitor environment

should be done. The right approach is to focus on how the decision was made and to be sure that the group used good decision processes and made thoughtful, well-considered decisions.

If managers strongly disagree with decisions and can clearly explicate to their subordinates why, then it may be reasonable to override some decisions, but this should be done only in extreme cases. There is no excuse, however, for a manager allowing decisions to be made based on a poor decision process or in a way that reflects biases or unfairness. If this is happening the manager needs to intervene and correct the decision process.

The second feature of the manager's role, which is particularly important in a high involvement organization, is the need to act more as a leader. Managers need to do more than simply carry out the day-to-day administrative duties of their job. Particularly crucial is the ability to articulate the management philosophy of the organization and the role of individuals in the organization. They need to provide a vision and manage symbols in ways that lead employees to understand the goals of the organization and be inspired by them (Bennis & Nanus, 1986). As has been pointed out in numerous books and articles on leadership, these skills are often difficult to develop in individuals.

TABLE 5.5 Reward System

Themes	Practices
Individualized	Skill based
Performance based	All-salary
Egalitarian	Gain sharing
Growth oriented	Profit sharing
	Ownership
	Flexible fringe benefits
	Participative appraisal
	Few perquisites

Nevertheless, a successful, participative organization needs some managers who are visionary, inspirational leaders.

Reward Systems

The reward system in a high involvement organization needs to emphasize and support the idea of information, knowledge, and power moving to the performer level. It can do this by rewarding individuals for developing their skills, by facilitating the movement of information downward in the organization, and finally by balancing power with rewards that depend on performance. It is particularly important that individuals who are empowered have rewards that are contingent upon how effectively they exercise their power. In a traditional organization it makes sense that individuals at the senior levels of management have a great deal of their compensation based upon the effectiveness of the organization. They are the ones that have the power to influence organizational performance and are clearly given that power. Once power has moved downward, it follows naturally that rewards for organizational performance should also move downward. Failure to do this constitutes a mismatch between power and rewards.

Table 5.5 lists a set of practices consistent with moving information, power, knowledge and rewards to lower levels. The major themes are

TABLE 5.6 Training Development

Themes	Practices
Lifetime learning	Economic education
Economic literacy	Team skills training
Team work	Skill assessments
Personal growth	Peer input
Understand the business	Problem-solving training
	Horizontal and vertical training

egalitarian, skill growth-oriented, individual choice, and—as much as possible—pay based on group and organization performance. Some of the practices listed are relatively new while others have been around for quite a while. For example, gain sharing, profit sharing, and all-salary work forces have been used for decades in some organizations (Lawler, 1981). Other practices such as skill-based pay and flexible benefits have been increasingly used in just the last 10 years. It is new, however, to combine these into a single reward system that is intended to support a high involvement management approach.

Training and Development

High involvement management by necessity places a strong emphasis on training and development. If information and power are going to be moved downward it is vital that the knowledge and skills to use them be moved downward as well. Thus in Table 5.6, which enumerates the education practices that are consistent with high involvement organization, there is an emphasis on all kinds of training. Not only do individuals need to understand the economics of business, they need to be provided with training that supports their understanding of the work process and the work flow. They also need to be trained so that they can participate in problem-solving groups, teams, and task forces. Finally, skill assessment is critical. It is the key administrative procedure that an organization needs in order to be assured that individuals are capable of exercising power and dealing with the information that they are given.

TABLE 5.7 Staffing

Themes	Practices
Careful	Realistic preview
Mutual commitment	Employment security
Must support the culture	Peer input
Personal growth	Extensive testing/interviewing
	Open job posting
	Test for technical and social skills
	Promotion from within

Staffing

Not everyone is capable of, or interested in, working in a high involvement organization. Estimates differ quite a bit on what percentage of the work force wants more challenge and responsibility in their jobs, but few dispute that not everyone does. Thus staffing decisions need to receive a great deal of attention.

As shown in Table 5.7, a number of selection practices need to be instituted that are designed to assure that individuals know what is expected of them and to assure that the organization has individuals who have the motivation and ability to succeed in a high involvement organization. The selection process needs to include not only a realistic preview of the work and the way the organization operates but an extensive testing procedure in which individuals are tested for their ability to do the job and also to handle the social and decision-making aspects of the organization. The realistic preview can be handled by having individuals do the work and be interviewed by work teams so that they have a sense of what it is like to operate in a team environment.

Once individuals are hired, then the key issues concern how promotions are handled and how job openings are filled. Here the emphasis is on participative decision making; peers are typically asked for their input into promotion and placement decisions and, of course, a strong emphasis is placed on promotion from within.

Finally, employment security and stability are stressed because of their congruence with asking individuals to make a substantial commitment to developing skills which are specific to their organization. High involvement organizations ask individuals to commit a great deal of their time, effort, and energy to developing an understanding of their own organization and the skills that are necessary to operate it. These skills may not be transferable and, in addition, they are difficult for an organization to build and replace. Thus a policy of high employment security and stability makes a great deal of sense both from the point of view of the organization, which needs to retain its valued human resources, and from the viewpoint of the individual who is being asked to develop skills that are perhaps difficult to develop and that may not be transferable to another organization.

Personnel Policies

Personnel policies need to support a high involvement approach, not just in their content but in the way they are developed. They are one area where even from the beginning most individuals can meaningfully participate in organizational decisions. Thus as is shown in Table 5.8, it is very important that employees participate in the design of the personnel policies and in their administration. This can best be done through policy committees, grievance committees, and other cross-sectional groups of employees.

Because of the emphasis in high involvement organizations on individual responsibility and trust, it follows that the personnel policies should allow individuals considerable choice. Thus whenever possible, practices such as flex time and telecommuting should be used. It is also important that the family responsibilities of employees be taken into account. A great deal is demanded of employees in high involvement organizations; thus help with child care, elder care, and other family responsibilities is very important.

Finally, as part of the process of getting individuals involved in the organization, it is helpful for the organization to emphasize social events which encourage interaction. In situations where the technology tends to isolate people, social events and social interaction situations are particularly important because they can help to develop a sense of community and group cohesiveness and offset the isolation produced by technology. There should also be recognition events which acknowledge outstanding performance on the part of the organization and individuals. The key is to give social reward and recognition for doing a good job.

TABLE 5.8 Personnel Policies

Themes	Practices
Participative design	Task force to develop personnel policies
Participative administration	Ongoing personnel committee
	Grievance committee
Individual choice	Flex time
	Telecommuting
Encourage social interaction	Celebrations
	Special events
	Activities that include family
Development oriented	Financial support for education
Support family	Maternity and paternity leaves
	Child care

Overview: High Involvement Management

Now that we have reviewed eight design areas, we can return to the issues of congruence or fit and the issue of how different high involvement is from traditional management. As a general rule, the practices described are congruent with an organization design which pushes information, knowledge, power, and rewards downward. Taken together these practices constitute a radical departure from traditional management and open up a number of interesting new research areas for organizational researchers. Not only are there numerous issues having to do with the effectiveness of such new practices as skill-based pay, flexible benefits, work teams, information technology, and employment security, there are perhaps even more issues concerning the interface between the different systems. Are the systems congruent with each other? Do they in fact support each other and lead to organizational effectiveness? These questions have not been answered, but they warrant research and potentially can lead organizational researchers into new areas and new research paradigms.

Quality of worklife impact of high involvement management

There is little systematic evidence concerning the impact of high involvement management on quality of worklife of employees. Attitude survey data on a case-by-case basis tends to show that employees are more satisfied when they have enriched jobs, participate in decisions, share in the financial gains of their organization, and so forth (Lawler, 1986; Sashkin, 1984). These results are extremely important and cannot be dismissed. They suggest strongly that most people prefer the kind of worklife that is present in the high involvement organization to the one that is present in traditional organizations.

It is frequently suggested that high involvement organizations have lower absenteeism rates, turnover rates, and grievance rates. Again, no systematic data are available to support this point, but case after case tends to support it (Guzzo, Jette, & Katzell, 1985; Katzell & Guzzo, 1983). This finding follows directly from the argument that high involvement work situations are more satisfying and rewarding to individuals.

Stress is the one area where high involvement organizations may have a negative impact on quality of worklife. This speculation rests on the argument that along with power and responsibility inevitably come stress and demands that not all employees are comfortable meeting and dealing with. Sometimes high involvement management leads, for example, to individuals working longer hours and, thus being away from their families more. Numerous workers have reported to me in interviews that they tend to take work problems home with them or, in essence, think more like managers and experience some of the stresses and strains associated with managerial roles.

No systematic evidence exists on whether or not high involvement organizations produce higher levels of stress and whether the stress is converted into physical health problems. The stress is a different kind of stress than that experienced by employees who are powerless and alienated from their work. One argument is that employees in high involvement work settings are in a better position to deal with stress than employees in traditional organizations (Karasek, 1979). Because highly involved employees have the power to act upon the pressures they feel and the demands they experience in their work, they can alleviate stress in a productive way. In any case, the whole impact of high involvement management on stress appears to be an area that is in need of a great deal of research.

Organizational effectiveness

High involvement management is an unproven approach to managing organizations. There are data that suggest it is promising, but much of this data is based on assessment of individual practices that are part of the overall model rather than tests of the overall model (see, e.g., Katzell & Guzzo, 1983). The simple fact is there are few organizations at present that practice the high involvement model.

Perhaps the best examples of high involvement management are represented by the new plants which have been started throughout the United States during the last 20 years (Lawler, 1978). These plants incorporate many of the practices and themes characteristic of the high involvement model. Similarly, some of the older participatively managed gain-sharing companies, such as Herman Miller and Donnelly Mirrors, are highly consistent with the high involvement model. The evidence from both the new plants and the participative gain-sharing plants suggests that they indeed have been quite successful. For example, Procter & Gamble says that its new involvement-oriented plants are 30-40% more productive than its traditional plants. As a result of this, it is in the process of converting all of its plants to the participative or, as they call it, technician model. Similarly, companies like Herman Miller have been very successful for decades using the high involvement model. Indeed, Herman Miller was recently rated one of the 10 best managed companies by *Fortune* magazine.

A recent survey by the Center for Effective Organizations in conjunction with the General Accounting Office showed increased adoption of high involvement management principles (Lawler, Ledford, & Mohrman, 1989). The respondents also stated that the adoption of high involvement management practices did lead to improved performance. The respondents, who are senior executives, also said they plan increased adoption of employee involvement practices because they felt it could give them a competitive advantage. This finding fits with work by Denison (1984) which shows that organizations that have participative cultures tend to show superior financial performance.

Conclusion

Three strategies have been outlined for improving the competitive ness of U.S. organizations. They differ radically in their implications for quality of worklife and, indeed, for the kind of work that will be left in the United States. The first strategy, doing the traditional better promises little change in the quality of worklife in the United States although it does potentially mean some improvement in organizational performance. The second strategy may well mean that many kinds of work end up being done outside the United States or in new locations within the United States. It also means the development of a new form of organization that has different jobs and that treats people very differently. Some job loss clearly is inevitable from the second strategy because of the education level and the high cost of doing certain kinds of work in the United States. It does raise questions, however, about what type of work will be left in the U.S. for individuals with low education levels and low desires for involvement and challenging jobs. They clearly will not have a role in organizations which strategically position themselves around the world based on local conditions. Organizations of this type are going to put their simple repetitive work in countries with low labor costs, not in the United States.

Finally, the high involvement organization seems to represent an important new way for organizations to operate in the United States. It rests on the optimistic assumption that there is nothing wrong with American work or with the United States as a place to do business, but there is something wrong with the way American organizations have been managed. It clearly is not appropriate for all organizations, work, or individuals, but it may have the effect of making work more satisfying for many individuals and perhaps making it possible for many organizations to operate effectively in the United States. In essence, it can end up retaining in the United States work which might otherwise be sent to other countries. More than any other approach, it takes the democratic participative characteristics of the American society and puts them inside the organization from a management system perspective. Thus it may represent a way for U.S. organizations to be congruent with societal values and at the same time be competitive internationally. At this point it is premature to declare this approach a success or one that ought to be widely emulated; clearly much more research and data are needed. Nevertheless, there are many reasons for optimism.

References

Bennis, W., & Nanus, B. (1986). *Leaders.* New York: Harper & Row.

Davis, S., & Lawrence, P. (1977). *Matrix.* Reading, MA: Addison-Wesley.

Denison, D. (1984). Bringing corporate culture to the bottom line. *Organizational Dynamics, 12,* (4), 4-22.

Galbraith, J. R. (1977). *Organization design.* Reading, MA: Addison-Wesley.

Grayson, C. J., & O'Dell, C. (1988). *A two-minute warning.* New York: Free Press.

Guzzo, R. A., Jette, R. A., & Katzell, R. A. (1985). The effect of psychologically based intervention programs on worker productivity: A meta-analysis. *Personnel Psychology, 38,* 275-291.

Hackman, J. R., & Oldham, G. R. (1980). *Work redesign.* Reading, MA: Addison-Wesley.

Johnston, R. & Lawrence, P. R. (1988). Beyond vertical integration—the rise of the value-adding partnership. *Harvard Business Review, 66*(4), 94-101.

Karasek, R. A., Jr. (1979). Job demands, job decision latitude, and mental strain: Implications for job redesign. *Administrative Science Quarterly, 24,* 285-308.

Katzell, R. A., & Guzzo, R. A. (1983). Psychological approaches to productivity improvement. *American Psychologist, 38,* 468-472.

Lawler, E. E. (1978). The new plant revolution. *Organizational Dynamics, 6* (3), 2-12.

Lawler, E. E. (1981). *Pay and organization development.* Reading MA: Addison-Wesley.

Lawler, E. E. (1986). *High involvement management.* San Francisco: Jossey-Bass.

Lawler, E. E., & Mohrman, S. A. (1985). Quality circles after the fad. *Harvard Business Review, 85* (1), 64-71.

Lawler, E. E., Ledford, G. E., & Mohrman, S. A. (1989). *Employee involvement in America.* Houston: American Productivity and Quality Center.

Ledford, G. E., Lawler, E. E., & Mohrman, S. A. (1988). The Quality Circle and its variations. In J. P. Campbell & R. J. Campbell (Eds.), *Productivity in organizations* (pp. 255-294). San Francisco: Jossey-Bass.

Miles, R. E., & Snow, C. (1986). Organization: New concepts for new form. *California Management Review, 28,* 62-73.

MacDuffie, J. P. (1988). The Japanese auto transplants: Challenges to conventional wisdom. *ILR Report, 26*(1), 12-18.

Majchrzak, A. (1988). *The human side of factory automation: Managerial and human resource strategies for making automation succeed.* San Francisco: Jossey-Bass.

McGregor, D. (1960). *The human side of enterprise.* New York: McGraw-Hill.

Nadler, D., & Tushman, M. (1988). *Strategic organization design.* Glenview, IL: Scott Foresman.

Peters, T. (1987). *Thriving on chaos.* New York: Knopf.

Sashkin, M. (1984). Participative management is an ethical imperative. *Organizational Dynamics, 12*(4), 5-23.

Servan-Schreiber, J. J. (1968). *The American challenge.* New York: Atheneum.

Work in America: Report of a special task force to the Secretary of Health, Education, and Welfare. (1973). Cambridge: MIT Press.

Zubhoff, S. (1988). *In the age of the smart machine.* New York: Basic Books.

6 Mergers, Acquisitions, and the Reformatting of American Business

DWIGHT HARSHBARGER

This chapter will discuss the problems and challenges of developi managers for the new organizational realities of mergers and acqui tions. These new realities have emerged from an important and f reaching change process that is now taking place in America. Its ba is in corporate boardrooms and financial institutions. Its princip activity is in the buying and selling of companies. Its immediate cons quences include the streamlining of management operations, the gai ing of economies of scale, and often the displacement of workers a managers.

A Global Perspective on American Business

If American business leaders have learned anything in the past d cade, it is that we live and work in a world economy (e.g., Wristo 1986). To remain economically healthy we must learn to be competiti on a scale we have never known before; leaner, and perhaps mean The stakes are high. They include long-term control over our cultur our economic future, and in all likelihood the quality of our way of lif

I currently work as a senior executive at Reebok International. Muc though not all, of the production of Reebok and its subsidiaries is do in the Far East. Over 50,000 workers there are employed by manufa turers under contract to produce Reebok products. I have visited fact ries throughout the Far East and have frequent contact with our sta who are based there.

As I learn firsthand about these cultures, the economics of offsho production, and the dynamics of developing nations, I am also learnin more about America. When friends and former colleagues discuss offshore production with me, they quickly jump to conclusions about the economic benefits of the "cheap labor" supposedly available overseas. While this once may have been the case, for most companies it is no longer a sufficient reason for offshore production.

A recent series in *The New Yorker* by James Lardner (1988a, 1988b) thoughtfully analyzed domestic versus offshore production in the apparel industry. Lardner concluded, somewhat sadly, that offshore production of apparel continues to grow, despite difficult management problems created by import-export quotas in producer countries, because the quality of apparel produced in the United States simply doesn't measure up to industry standards.

Lardner's observations are consistent with my experiences in Korean manufacturing plants and my observations about the intensity of the work ethic among Korean employees. They work harder, longer and with greater discipline than I have seen in most American manufacturing plants. This work ethic begins early in life. High school students, for example, are expected to get no more than four hours of sleep a night. They are also expected to hold full-time jobs, live in dormitories, and attend school after completing a day's work in a factory.

The earnings of Korean footwear factory workers, principally in jobs that do not require extensive training and advanced skills, are now approaching U.S. levels of pay for similar jobs. In the production of athletic footwear, the differences in labor costs between Korea and the U.S. are marginal.

America is further disadvantaged by antiquated work rules, largely brought about through union contracts. These lead to the overstaffing of the workplace, thus lowering productivity per person and driving up costs. In fact, when American and Far Eastern workers' productivity are compared under similar workplace rules, the present productivity differences favoring the East disappear (Drucker, 1988).

Beyond all these factors, there is an offshore labor force of substantial size waiting to be employed. They bring with them the work ethic and its corollary, productivity, which are so important to a competitive advantage.

It is unsettling that these conditions—production quality, productivity, and labor supply—so necessary for business health are so difficult to find in the U.S. Moreover, the countries where these factors are simultaneously present are our competitors in a world economy.

Perhaps we had better take a long look at ourselves and think hard about the new realities of our economic world. Competing there is likely to require levels of stamina, skills, and drive that are unprecedented. It is also likely to require a lean and highly effective management overhead for companies that hope to survive.

There are many ways of making companies leaner and more competitive in the world marketplace, as Lawler has noted in Chapter 5. But one of the more socially significant methods to become prominent during the last decade has been the merger.

The Reformatting of the Management of American Companies: Mergers, Acquisitions, and Takeovers

In recent years the business press has reported extensively on mergers, acquisitions, and takeovers (or "M&As" for short) in publicly traded companies. Prior to 1980 the attention given M&As tended to focus on the organizational and product fit of the new company with the old. Later, researchers looked at the longer-term consequences of attempts at growth through acquisition during this period (e.g., Louis, 1982; Colby, 1986), concluding that 50% to 80% of the merged companies studied failed to perform consistent with financial projections.

In the late 1970s and early 1980s, high rates of inflation, major changes in tax laws, and the volatility of the oil industry set the stage for a qualitatively new approach to the M&A business. In the face of these changes, the current market value of large and complex companies became difficult to determine. For a variety of reasons many companies were undervalued; that is, their stock prices did not reflect the true underlying economic value of the corporation. Some divisions of a company might be positively affected by inflated prices and costs. Other parts might be adversely affected, depending on their array of products, their relationship to the oil industry, and the quality of their management, including management's ability to assess trends in an uncertain economic marketplace. A careful and cash-rich purchaser of companies could find numerous opportunities for gain. Many did.

In 1980 there were approximately 1,500 mergers of publicly traded companies with assets totaling $1 million or more. This was up slightly over the 1,400 M&As in 1979. The total value of these transactions was about $32 billion in 1980. (Note that neither these data, nor those that follow, include the mergers of privately held companies.) During the period 1981 to 1983 the number of acquisitions increased, then decreased slightly, but stayed in the 2,200-2,300 range of M&As per year. The total value of these transactions each year actually decreased from approximately $67 billion in 1981 to just $52 billion in 1983.

Then all hell broke loose. If 1983 was the year when America broke out of its economic recession, then 1984 was the year when American business really began to be bought and sold. A list of companies on the New York Stock Exchange assumed the form of a supermarket shopping list. In 1984 the number of M&As of companies with assets of $1 million or more jumped to approximately 3,150; continued to rise to 4,300 in 1986; then tailed off slightly but remained over 3,700 in 1987.

In 1984 alone, the value of these transactions increased two and one-half times, from $52 billion to approximately $125 billion. This accelerating curve continued through 1986 when the value of M&As reached $204 billion. There was a decrease in 1987 to just over $167 billion, still well over the 1985 level of $145 billion ("1987 profile," 1988). Observers who are close to the M&A action are predicting that M&As in 1988 will be at an all-time high ("Takeover Pace," 1988).

During this period of accelerated M&A activity, an important qualitative change occurred in the descriptions of M&As in the press. The term takeover, or hostile takeover, began to be used with such frequency that the process it referred to became a lifelike thing, one to be feared and fought. The term *takeover* refers to the acquisition of a company against the wishes of its management, often leading to political campaigns by management to garner the support and votes of more than 50% of the shares outstanding. While the process itself was not new, its frequency of occurrence began to transform the ways we looked at M&As.

And, to make observers of American business just a bit more cynical, the process of greenmail began to be prominently reported. Its prominence did not come from newness; rather, from its increased frequency and the drama associated with the large fortunes being acquired through the use of greenmail by corporate raiders such as Carl Icahn.

In *greenmail*, a hostile tender is made for a company. The target company, to end the threat of an acquisition hostile to management, agrees to buy the shares now owned by the potential acquirer at a price well above their current market value. In exchange, the would-be purchaser agrees to go away and leave the company alone. It is corporate poker with high stakes.

An Example

Consider the recent acquisition of Federated Department Stores by Robert Campeau, the Canadian businessman. After a 10-week struggle to outbid or outmaneuver R. H. Macy and Co., Campeau and Federated agreed on a $6.6 billion sale price. With the completion of the purchase, Campeau became the fourth largest retailer in America, trailing only Sears, K Mart and Wal-Mart.

The transaction was complex, as one might expect in a deal of this magnitude. Some highlights are listed below ("Campeau at last," 1988).

- Up to $1.8 billion in high-yield bonds guaranteed by Campeau
- 50% of Campeau's American holding company pledged to a financial backer in exchange for a $480 million loan
- Federated's I. Magnin and Bullock's-Bullock's Wilshire divisions sold to Macy for $1.1 billion
- $60 million of Macy's expenses paid by Campeau
- Federated's Brooks Brothers sold to Marks and Spencer
- Other Federated divisions, such as Filene's, Main Street, Foley's and Filene's Basement appear likely to be sold in order to raise cash to pay for the purchase

Real estate, products, programs, and people: all are in transition, though with an uncertain destination. A friend told me of once meeting an acquaintance rushing down a street in a rural West Virginia town. As the man approached, the friend yelled, "Where are you going?" Pausing only briefly, the man replied, "How should I know? I am on my way!"

The Mergers and Acquisitions Business

The complex transactions described above are made possible by an infrastructure in the financial-legal-securities communities. It is this infrastructure that comprises the core of the mergers and acquisitions business and is itself forming a new community. The Campeau-Federated deal alone is estimated to have generated approximately $500 million in fees for M&A advisory firms. In part, they are as follows ("Wall Street Enjoys," 1988):

First Boston Corporation	$50–60 million
Shearson Lehman Hutton	$23 million
Goldman, Sachs	$15–20 million
Hellman and Friedman	$15–20 million
Kidder Peabody	$15 million
Drexel Burnham Lambert	$15 million
Wasserstein, Perella	$10 million
Citibank, Sumitomo et al.	$43.5 million
Arbitrage firms, including Salomon Brothers, Oppenheimer, Prudential-Bache, Kellner, di Leo	$300 million
Citibank, Bankers Trust, and Manufacturers Hanover	$30 million
Paine Webber and Dillon Read	$12 million

While the above list is incomplete, it begins to reflect some of the scope and complexity of the M&A business. Remember, though it was large and complex, the Campeau-Federated deal was only a single transaction.

The securities industry produced about $3.5 billion in profits in 1987. One billion dollars came from M&As. Approximately 50,000 people are now employed in investment banks, commercial banks and law firms to do work that is directly related to M&As. Beyond this there are management consultants, economists, insurers, and a host of other specialized professionals who earn their living from M&As.

This new industry's growing efforts are fueled by substantial borrowing, tough minded business analysis, and a corporate search for competitive advantages. It is founded on a belief in the future and an optimism about being able to run businesses more efficiently and more profitably than was done by prior management.

Don't think of the mergers and acquisitions business as a class of business or business practices. Think of it as a new industry, complete with its own newly emerging specialty skills among practitioners, and cumulatively having its own industrywide learning curve. While this new species of executives can ply its growing competencies only when armed with cash and vast borrowing power, the consistently increasing number of M&As suggests that it is becoming more and more skilled in doing its business.

Some Consequences of M&A Reformatting

Calculating the numbers of people affected by M&As in the United States is a difficult and imperfect process. One manufacturing company with $200 million in sales may employ about 2,000 people; a ratio of one employee per thousand dollars in sales. A company with over $1 billion in sales, but doing its manufacturing under contract off shore, may employ the same number of people, though an additional 50,000 may work for the off shore companies who are subcontractors. A rule of thumb in banking is one employee per million dollars in assets; a bank with $1 billion in assets would have 1000 employees. Other businesses may be more or less capital intensive.

In the absence of hard information on people employed in acquired and acquirer companies, the best that can be done is to make some estimates. These estimates must come from a choice about the ratio of people employed to dollar assets or sales of these companies. Taking the year 1985, with M&As of companies whose assets totaled $139 billion, I estimated that 750,000 to 1.4 million people were employed by companies on either end of an acquisition (Harshbarger, 1987). While it is possible to make different assumptions and reach somewhat different numbers of people, whatever numbers are calculated will be substantial. It is no small problem. Then, if these numbers are placed in a cumulative running total, year after year, and examined in terms of the percent of the work force in America touched by the M&A process, the size of the problem begins to become evident.

The human drama resulting from M&As becomes even more complex when we begin to examine the as yet sketchy data on job loss after an acquisition. Following acquisitions during the period from 1981 to 1986, 500,000 executives lost jobs they had held for more than three years. 30% of them were still unemployed two years later. Among blue-collar workers approximately 35% were unemployed two years after the acquisition (Nulty, 1987).

Lamalie Associates reported that during the period from 1980 to 1984, approximately 50% of all executives in acquired companies left within one year after the acquisition. An additional 25% planned to leave in the second year. Among executives leaving their companies after acquisitions, 50% termed the acquisition hostile, regardless of its formal definition ("Fast Exits," 1986).

While these statistics are compelling, a bit of autobiography may provide a deeper understanding of the potential human impact of

M&As. In 1981 I became Vice President of Human Resources at Sealy, Inc. I was there when the company went through a hostile takeover.

In the spring of 1987, the takeover of Sealy was complete. It was a very personal and painful process that has been written about elsewhere (Harshbarger, 1987). The management of the new company discussed some career options that were open to me if I stayed on. None of these, however, would have continued me in my former role or as a key officer in the company.

I had no other job offers. But too many fundamentals in the culture I had helped build were being disassembled by the new owners. Too many compromises were called for. I decided to leave the company.

To be sure, my departure was economically softened by a reasonably attractive severance package. But such things consist of time and money, and both are soon gone. You are then left with your skills, your wits, and—if you are lucky,—your health. But no job.

Like most recently severed executives, I began the process of networking and sending out resumes. Friends in corporate posts as well as in the consulting business faced the difficult task of saying, "Sorry, but we don't have any openings just now." In short, go away. After a few dozen of these kinds of experiences, at a time when I didn't need them, I began to doubt if I was the competent professional that I thought I was.

I saw developing what I feared would be a long, arduous, and stressful pattern of searching. My fantasy of the world rushing to offer me new positions was ended. As I wondered about my professional competence, I saw changes beginning to occur in me, changes I did not like. So, quite simply, I said to hell with this and began my own business, a management consulting practice.

My new venture very quickly took root and began to grow. Much of my work was with the corporation that had taken over Sealy. And over the months of 1987, I experienced professional challenges from a position I had never been in before: No guarantees. If you work, you earn and eat. If you don't, tough. I worked hard and ate reasonably well.

Then my career took another unexpected turn near the end of 1987. A friend and colleague of many years had begun consulting with Reebok. He assessed organizational needs there that he thought I might be helpful in addressing. I joined the company in January, 1988, in my present position.

I do not believe my experience was unique. Following my departure from Sealy, in the course of my consulting work and more recently at Reebok, I have interviewed numerous other executives who have come through an acquisition or takeover. My interviews were not part of a systematic examination of the effects of M&As on executives; the interviews were focused on appraisals for purposes of management development or selection for a key position. However, my fascination with the acquisition experience led me to use the opportunity to pursue questions about the meaning of the experience to executives and its impact on their lives.

The following representative comments suggest something about the psychological consequences of experiencing an acquisition. Remember, these were competent, successful and highly placed executives.

> "If I ever again work in a company and hear serious talk of our being acquired, I'm heading for the door."
>
> "I'm okay most of the time. But I never know what's coming. It's like I'm on an emotional roller coaster and I never know when the ride is to begin."
>
> "I still have my job, but it's not the same. The people are nice, but their values are different. I like my work, but it's not the same."
>
> "I've been president of major divisions in two corporations that have been acquired. You can get rich going through it, but it's not worth it. I just want to build something and see it grow and be successful."
>
> "Trust nobody."

I haven't interviewed people who have come through M&As and have been either at lower levels of management or less competent than the executives described above. However, I have known some and have talked with them. They had little good to say about M&As in particular or business in general: Survive. Get what you can when you can. And, in a few cases, get it any way you can. One guy wished he could be like Carl Icahn.

We often define ourselves in terms of our work. It becomes who we are. Ask someone the question "What sort of work do you do?" and listen carefully to the answer. It will probably begin "I am a. . . ." The question was about work as an activity. The answer was about a state of being. An existential definition of oneself. No small matter. And when this thing called work is radically changed, or worse, lost, we feel pain. A part of ourselves has been taken away.

The Paradoxes of Work in the World of M&As

We all have ways of thinking about our work lives and planning for the future. Those of us who are managers anticipate some sort of progression in our careers, look toward the challenges of new assignments and managerial problems with a mixture of excitement and trepidation, and assume we will have a retirement package waiting at the end of our career paths. We pray that we will remain in good health, though we are protected by employer-sponsored health and disability plans should things go wrong.

For the half million executives who lost their jobs because of M&As between 1981 and 1986, these assumptions about the future were blown away. Worse, their displacement did not occur because of something that they had done. They just didn't fit. They weren't needed any more. (Note: People close to the labor movement may be watching all this with amusement. From their perspective, management must seem to be doing to itself—that is, layoffs of able-bodied managers—what they have watched it do to laborers for many years.)

It seems reasonable to make the assumption that, following an acquisition, people who are asked to remain with the new company are likely to be those who are competent in their jobs, have unique skills, or both. In addition, people who are employed by the acquirer are likely to have more job security than people in the acquired company. The latter feeling grows out of the American preference for viewing such experiences as acquisitions and takeovers as business versions of athletic contests, with wining and loosing teams. Winning, or acquiring, can be a lot of fun. Losing, or being acquired, hurts.

Prime Computer, a minicomputer maker in Massachusetts, recently completed a hostile takeover of Computervision Corporation. Prime then announced the elimination of 700 jobs from *its own* work force ("Prime Computer," 1988). So much for our assumptions about the security associated with acquiring and being a winner.

As the reformatting of business occurs, things will alternately seem to make sense and then be unfathomable. The dilemmas and paradoxes of worklife will become more visible. They also will become more disturbing, for it will become apparent that not only are there no easy answers, often there are no answers at all.

Two of these paradoxes are likely to be particularly troubling to managers, for they involve behaviors and emotions that are at the core of the relationship between individual managers and their companies.

1. The paradox of community and commitment

Managers have long been asked to make full commitments to their companies, to build strong work groups, and to help build the larger culture and strengthen its values. Successful careers, we quickly learn, are built by self-sacrifice and by putting the company first.

In ever larger numbers, managers are learning that having done this diligently and well is no guarantee of anything. If after an acquisition a department is eliminated, its managers are likely to be gone. Afterward, as the psychological fog clears, managers wonder about the commitments they made and the reciprocity they thought was part of their relationship with the company. In the film *Network News* there is a wonderfully sensitive series of scenes portraying life during a major cutback of staff in the network's Washington bureau. After the head of the news division terminates a long-term employee, he places his arm around the shoulder of the man and rather unctuously says, "If there is ever anything I can do for you, please let me know." The employee dryly replies, "Well, you can die soon."

The cynicism that often characterizes attitudes of people who have been through M&As, particularly takeovers, is a byproduct of this paradox; that is, it becomes a way of protecting oneself from a dilemma in life that is so complex it seems impossible to understand. As more and more people live through M&As, this cynicism is becoming more prevalent. It also travels with managers to their new organizations.

2. The paradox of belief in the corporate future

We do not approach our work as if there is no tomorrow. Tomorrow is very important. If we can't assume it to be there, then work—indeed, life itself—takes on a radically different meaning.

People assume a job future for themselves and a corporate future for their companies as a normal part of worklife. There are psychological promissory notes that are exchanged between individual managers and the corporate employer. While these notes may be little more than expressions of good faith in each other and a common future, they are an important part of the social infrastructure that holds the corporate body together.

When M&As occur, these assumptions about the future are at best in question, and often violated. The belief in a corporate future, so essential to each person in approaching work, now becomes a major vulnerability. Having made a substantial investment of their lives in companies, individual managers suddenly find their investments are all at risk. It is not easy to accept the new reality that suddenly there are very real potentials for divorce. The unexpected termination of any employee sends shockwaves into the life of that person, and lesser waves into the culture of an organization. The negative effects of these waves are minimized to the extent the termination was for performance reasons. But when tens, even hundreds, of people lose their jobs in the acquisition of a single company, and tens of thousands of managers lose jobs in the companies acquired in a given year in America, the impact on people and corporate cultures is substantial.

Learning to Cope with Reformatting

Up to now the picture painted of M&As reflects the darker side of business life: hostile takeovers, greenmail, personal loss, and psychological pain. However, M&As are serious business. They occur when careful, often conservative students of the companies in question see more effective and potentially profitable ways to operate them. Many M&As are not only inevitable but desirable.

Thus, the issue is not one of stopping M&As, or making them more difficult or expensive. The issue is one of learning how to learn from them—about business and about ourselves. If we become serious students of the process, we might learn how to manage companies, develop people, and acquire or be acquired in ways that, though painful, better prepare us all for new realities.

Also, M&As are part of a larger trend. The ownership and management of American business is going through a process of being reformatted. In reformatted companies, management layers will be fewer, management ranks thinner, and challenges to managers greater than has been known in the past. To do all this and be competitive, managers will need to be personally tougher, more responsive to opportunities and challenges, and more secure in their sense of who they are than ever before.

The pain of an acquisition or takeover is hard to bear. But the mos meaningful of life's lessons seem to have a lot of pain in them. An from these lessons, we learn. Then change. Ernest Hemingway onc noted, "Life sometimes breaks people. And when they mend, often the are stronger in the broken places." The reformatting of American busi ness will be painful. And when it is over we will be stronger.

The personal trauma and psychological pain accompanying the cul ture shock of acquisitions and takeovers has received considerabl recent attention (e.g., Colby, 1986; Harshbarger, 1987; Marks & Mervis, 1985, 1986; Nulty, 1987; Pritchett, 1985; and Schweiger Ivancevich & Power, 1987). In attempting to understand the psycholog ical reactions of people to potential and real job loss and career insecu rities, researchers of takeovers have frequently used the five-stag sequential model of death and grieving developed by Kubler-Ros (1969) to describe the human drama surrounding reactions to the take over process. Those of us who have experienced the pain of a takeove and the loss of a job know firsthand the meaning of Kubler-Ross' theory in the context of business life.

It is a short step from observations and theories about personal los to programs and practices designed to help people adaptively respon to the experience. Short-term and crisis-oriented counseling programs often used to help people work through the grief associated with othe forms of loss in their lives, would seem appropriate—indeed, necessary However, treatment services that go beyond short-term counseling are the wrong strategy for employees and for our culture.

There will always be a market for treatment services. But, as has been found in building programs of public education and community devel opment, the treatment and remediation of problems is not the best path to a healthy and adaptive future for people or for our culture. Rather we must learn how to make these services unnecessary. We must learn how to build cultures that produce competent people: people who are prepared to deal with the unexpected in their work lives, including the trauma of job loss.

The Rise of the Corporate Culture Concept

A few years ago the book *In Search of Excellence* (Peters & Water man, 1982) captured the imagination of the business world. The authors described what they viewed as well-run companies and the values and practices that were part of corporate life in those companies. About the same time Deal and Kennedy (1983) published an applied anthropological view of corporate cultures and described how those cultures affected the conduct of the business; it was also a success. Both books moved through the business world with the speed of a grass fire on a dry and windy Dakota prairie.

There have been later treatments of these and similar themes (e.g., Peters & Austin, 1985; Peters, 1988), but among working managers these other books haven't had the same impact on altering how they think about the fundamentals of managing as did the *Excellence* book.

Today, with historical hindsight, the cultural context in which those books were published has become as fascinating as the books themselves. 1984, a year when company presidents were handing out Peters and Waterman's book like popcorn, was the year when the number of M&As nearly doubled, and the asset value of those transactions virtually tripled from the preceding year. At a time when managers in personnel, industrial relations, and human resources were discovering corporate values and Peters and Waterman's road map to the future, the terrain on which they travelled was being transformed. Their companies were being purchased, disassembled, and reassembled at an unprecedented rate.

The intellectual attraction of the new, value-oriented view of corporate life may have had its emotional roots in a growing awareness among these managers that something was wrong, and their faith that there was a way to do things right. They accorded Peters and Waterman the status of high priests of corporate cultures, and the task of defining values in their respective companies became an important priority for human resource professionals. In turn, these professionals were accorded a new status by their fellow employees.

But the world quickly changes. In 1985 a CEO whose company had fallen on less profitable times said to me, "That values bullshit was okay when we were making money. Now we've got to get serious about the business." The bloom had fallen from the human resource rose.

Some Old Ideas for New Times: Building a
Culture of Managerial Competence

I believe that individuals and organizations can best prepare for the turbulent years ahead by focusing on the creation of *competence-*

producing environments; that is, those in which people learn adaptive skills. They come to know their skills are adaptive, thus helpful to themselves *and* the organization, because they learn about the consequences of their behavior. A healthy culture is one in which people find it rewarding to experience their own learning curves and participate in the learning curves of others. B. F. Skinner (1953, 1971) has repeatedly advised us on what needs to be done in order to accomplish this task. Gilbert (1978) has given us an articulate description of how to go about it. I offer four simple, guiding principles:

1. Focus explicitly on performance. Good intentions, positive attitudes and people who want to try are not enough. In fact, they are antithetical to sound performance management. Managers who legitimize their incomplete, often substandard, performance by describing how they "tried" are fooling themselves and performing a disservice to their companies.

Establish organized and positively sanctioned ways of reviewing performance; not just an annual review, but frequent reviews of projects and daily work. Make it part of the daily life of the company. Do it in a way that helps people learn about themselves. Work with them and challenge yourself to find ways to do things more competently. Share in the pain and excitement of learning.

2. Establish clear expectations about performance. A manager's job is to manage. It is likely to be done best when the people being managed have a clear understanding about what is expected of them.

Substantial time and energy will need to be devoted to this if it is to be done well. One of the luxuries and, simultaneously, hazards of being in the managerial ranks is that one has considerable power over the sanctioning of expectations and the definition of reality. When a subordinate fails to understand what is expected, a manager can define the problem as "his problem, not mine." This makes life easier for managers in the short term; however, an organization which sanctions this as a norm for managers is heading for problems in the long term.

Do simple things. Do them well. "Here's what I expect. . . ." Then a discussion. "These are the standards I use in looking at the quality of your work. . . ." Then a discussion. "I see the needs of the company as follows. . . ." Then a discussion. A small investment in this process can pay enormous dividends to the manager, the subordinate, and the company.

3. Both a teacher and a student be. Most managers define their roles as containing some responsibility for teaching or training subordinates.

What many managers fail to include are their own responsibilities to be students and to learn from their people. As a consequence, the axis of communication between manager and subordinate tilts toward an up-down angle, with no surprises about who is on the upper end of it.

We know these people well. They were the teachers we didn't like when we were in school, and they are the managers we don't want to work for now. Unfortunately there are a lot of them. But fortunately they, too, have managers. Everybody works for somebody. And that somebody can establish expectations and set performance standards that are designed to alter these practices in a positive way.

Learning can be fun. Teaching can be fun. The most effective work groups and the best managers I have known have discovered this. They mix it up and shift roles from teacher to student and back again: managers and subordinates, together, involved in problem solving and learning.

4. Hold managers accountable for people development. Some organizations do this. Others leave it up to "the personnel people." A few assume that people must do it for themselves. However it is done, including the use of internal and external training programs, individual managers must look at their people and, with each of them, plan a program for individual development.

When a manager is fortunate enough to have bright, competent, and highly motivated people, this is easily accomplished. It is the people who are marginal performers that require time-consuming hard work. But these are the very people who, if put on track and given some encouragement, can make all the difference in a company.

To be effective, managers need skills that go far beyond a technical command of their respective disciplines. Not only must they have good coaching skills, they must find the coaching process rewarding. Many do. Unfortunately, many don't. They shouldn't be managers.

Finally, managers' accountability for people development should include the assignment of readying one or more candidates to succeed themselves. This concept should be taken further: No manager is to be promoted until a subordinate is ready or a search completed, with external searches receiving sparing use. If, over time, a manager can't develop people from within, then the company has either the wrong people or a manager who is lacking in important skills.

How do we prepare managers for new realities? We do these things: Give honest feedback. Communicate expectations. Share in teaching and learning. Take responsibility for developing people.

Done well, we will create competent people and companies. Paradoxically, these companies are likely to be among those most attractive for acquisitions because their people will be good at what they do, including making a profit. And people coming up through these cultures are not likely to fear an acquisition. They will know who they are and what they do well, and they will have a realistic view of their market value and future career options.

The Problem of Individual Security

One problem continues to concern me as I assess the impact of acquisitions and takeovers on the fabric of corporate life. It has to do with individual managers and how they prepare to cope with an ever more uncertain organizational future.

Of all the things that are lost when managers are displaced because of acquisitions, the one that is most troublesome and threatening is the loss of financial security in later years. It affects both the managers and their families.

Relatively few people in corporate life view themselves as modern-day Horatio Algers. The security of organizational life is valued by many, perhaps most, employees and managers. An important part of that security is a company's programs aimed at providing income after retirement. When these programs are threatened, or lost, people are frightened. It is a major concern for families, particularly when there are other problems, such as adult dependent children or family members with poor health. It is a fear that causes people to lie awake at night.

Colleges and universities, faced with the retirement problems of increasingly transient faculties, solved this problem years ago. TIAA and CREF-based retirement programs became transferable across employers; as a result, a college faculty member might have multiple employers over the course of a career, but a single retirement program building equity for the retirement years. It has been a successful program.

We should examine alternatives for creating similar retirement program options for employees of corporations. Though the problem is complex, it is solvable. For example, employees could be given a choice: participate in the pension or profit-sharing program of their employer, or direct that those same monies be contributed to a multi-employer retirement/investment fund.

There are a host of technical issues that come with this proposal. How would such a fund be managed? Should it be organized by industry? Would its management be shared by existing investment institutions whose financial power is already a source of concern to financial analysts? What are reasonable investment goals? There are many, many more possible questions.

I am not a financial expert. I only know that we have a very real and important human concern. It grows out of changes that are taking place in our culture and are likely to continue well into the future. And there *is* a model for solving the problem that has been successfully used in one industry. I recommend it for serious examination.

Preparing Reformatted Organizations for New Realities: Succession Planning

If people and organizations are to be readied for a reformatted future and the new realities it may bring, then attention must be given to the process of succession planning. Succession planning, by its very nature, is an imperfect process. It requires that managers have completed sound appraisals of their people, the business needs of the organization, and the likely realities of the future. The first two can be done with a modicum of skill and accuracy, but defining the future is at best an educated guess.

While it is surprising how many organizations give little more than lip service to succession planning, those that take it seriously typically focus on three principal elements of a succession planning program: periodic review, programs of managerial development, and identifying future leadership.

1. Periodic review. At least once a year top management of a division or corporation should convene and review the current performance of incumbents in key positions and the developmental status of their potential successors. Some names are removed from the lists and new ones are added. These reviews are likely to take a couple of days and often lead to thoughtful and productive discussions about the possible alternative futures for the organization.

2. Accountable programs of management development. The people who are charged with setting policies and priorities in place for building people for the future, principally the participants in the periodic review, must then hold themselves and their subordinates accountable for pro-

grams to develop people—all the developmental processes described i
the prior section of this paper.

In the life of many companies it is at this point that things begin t
go wrong. What begins as accountable managerial behavior is trans
formed into good intentions. This typically happens when pressin
financial needs receive the immediate attention of executives, and tha
promised review session focusing on the longer-term developmenta
needs of a key executive is postponed. At first this may occur becaus
of unexpected events—often crises—in the business. Later it become
a pattern, one that otherwise competent executives, including humai
resource executives, actively support. It makes their work lives mucl
easier, at least until harvest time.

3. Identifying the company's future leadership. Sound successioi
planning has two objectives. The first is to find and develop people wh
will competently manage the organization. In selecting them, manager
should be targeted who can be described as *value added* people. Tha
is, there is a unique and added value in the problem-solving skills an
contributions of each of them, a creative or innovative approach t
problems. While no one is indispensable, these are people who canno
be easily replaced.

The second objective is to find people whose value added include
leadership: managers who challenge established methods or values
people who chart new directions; managers who develop strong team
and build people; and the people who, when they were kids, wer
consistently asked by their peers to lead because everybody seemed t
play better and have more fun when they were around.

The assessment of leadership is perhaps the most difficult assessmen
to make in the process of succession planning. It is also the mos
important. Executives, and perhaps businesses, typically fail but no
because they don't understand the technical aspects of their missions
It happens because they fail to lead.

Conclusion

American business has entered a period of reformatting; a shifting
and sifting in corporate ownership and the structure of its management
When it emerges from this period it will be substantially changed
Companies that survive will be more efficient, have greater economie
of scale, and be more effective than before. If successful, U.S. compa

nies will become stronger and more competitive players in the world economy than they have been.

Between the now of the present and then of the future, there lie the challenges of change: all the things that must be done to go from here to there, all the pain, and all the opportunities of personal and organizational change. It will not be easy. Faint hearts will not travel well on this road. But it is a trip that must be taken.

The debilitating consequences of M&As, real though they are, are painful principally because they violate our expectations about what we thought life was going to be. We forget that many of the important things we take for granted, including retirement programs, have come about relatively recently.

Managers who bury themselves in grief over the inequities and unfairness brought about by a takeover and loss of a job will not adapt well to the new realities they will face. Rather, managers will best meet these challenges by developing levels of psychological resilience and personal competence that they have not know before. Outward Bound could become a better curriculum for the development of managers than what is taught in many graduate programs. Personally challenging and feedback-rich environments will be essential in order for people to learn about themselves and test the limits of their skills and stamina.

As we come through the reformatting of our business culture, we must renew our commitments to ourselves and to work as an opportunity to learn, even when it has the potential to be unexpectedly taken away from us. Nobody ever said life was fair. Just an opportunity to learn. And contribute.

I'd like to conclude by respectfully dedicating this chapter to J. Robert Daniel, former superintendent of Spencer State Hospital, an old and underfunded institution in West Virginia.

Bob was appointed to his position by the governor. Because of this he was often reflective about his job future, and the risks that come with the electoral process. He estimated that, at best, an eight-year horizon—two terms—was all the time he had to turn around the culture of the institution. There was much to be done. And between the beginning and the end of those eight years, there also were the problems of internecine wars between the differing factions in state government. "If one doesn't get you, the other one will," he commented.

Once, reflecting on the difficulties of managing an aging institution with an inadequate budget, in a political system that has been periodically corrupt and never a model for state government anywhere, Bob said, "I am going to do what I think is right in running this place. If they don't agree with me, they can show me a better way. If it's right, I'll do it. If it isn't, I won't. The governor and his people in the statehouse can make a choice. Do it my way, or fire me."

Then, after a pause, Bob taught a lesson in living. He pointed to the front door of the institution and spoke slowly and forcefully as he said, "We all make compromises, but you can't live your life that way. If need be, I am ready to walk out that door and down the street. Before the day is over, I'll be making a living. I may be selling cars, but it will be honest work."

Bob Daniel was willing to take personal risks to achieve what he believed to be managerially and morally right. He knew who he was and where he wanted to take his organization. Should it go awry for the wrong reasons, he was willing to walk out the door. One day, he did just that.

The reformatting of American business will require that we, like Bob, focus our commitments and be prepared to act on them. If, because of a reformatting, our commitments are brought into question or conflict, we must do what is right. In the extreme, that may mean walking out the door. Difficult though it may be for us personally, it is the stuff of which integrity is made. We will need a lot of it if we hope to control our future.

References

Campeau at last gets federated—now can he make a go of it? (1988, April 4). *Wall Street Journal*.

Colby, L. (1986, June 16). Managing the human side of a merger or acquisition. *Personnel Management: Policies and Practices* (pp. 393-397). Inglewood Cliffs, NJ:Prentice Hall Information Service.

Deal, T. E., & Kennedy, A. A. (1983). *Corporate cultures*. Reading, MA: Addison-Wesley.

Drucker, P. (1988, August 4). Workers' hands bound by tradition. *Wall Street Journal*.

Fast exits for executives. (1986, March-April). *Mergers and Acquisitions*, p. 21.

Gilbert, T. (1978). *Human competence*. New York: McGraw-Hill.

Harshbarger, D. (1987). Takeover: A tale of loss, change and growth. *The Academy of Management Executives, Vol. 1*(3), 337-341.

Kubler-Ross, E. (1969). *On death and dying*. New York: Macmillan.

Lardner, James. (1988, January 11). Annals of business: The sweater trade—I. *The New Yorker*, pp. 39-73.

Lardner, James. (1988, January 18). Annals of business: The sweater trade—II. *The New Yorker*, pp. 57-73.

Louis, A. (1982, May 3). The bottom line on ten big mergers. *Fortune*, pp. 84-89.

Marks, M. L., & Mervis, P. (1985, Summer). Merger syndrome: Stress and uncertainty. *Mergers and Acquisitions,* pp. 50-55.

Marks, M. L., & Mervis, P. (1986, January-February). Merger syndrome: Management by crisis, Part II. *Mergers and Acquisitions*, pp. 70-76.

Nulty, P. (1987, March 2). Pushed out at 45—now what? *Fortune*, pp. 26-34.

Peters, T. (1988). *Thriving on chaos*. New York: Alfred A. Knopf.

Peters, T., & Austin, N. (1985). *The leadership difference*. New York: Random House.

Peters, T., & Waterman, R. (1982). *In search of excellence*. New York: Harper & Row.

Prime Computer eliminating 700 from work force. (1988, May 12). *Boston Globe*.

Pritchett, P. (1985). *After the merger: Managing the shockwaves*. New York: Dow Jones-Irwin.

Schweiger, D. M., Ivancevich, J. M., and Power, F. R. (1987, May). Executive actions for managing human resources before and after acquisitions. *Academy of Management Executives*, pp. 127-138.

Skinner, B. F. (1953). *Science and human behavior*. New York: Macmillan.

Skinner, B. F. (1971). *Beyond freedom and dignity*. New York: Alfred A. Knopf.

Takeover pace is seen picking up in 1988. (1988, January 4). *Wall Street Journal*.

Wall Street enjoys "present" from Federated. (1988, April 5). *Boston Globe*.

Wriston, W. (1986, January-February). The world according to Walter. *Harvard Business Review*, pp. 65-69.

1987 profile of mergers and acquisitions. (1988, May-June). *Mergers and Acquisitions*, pp. 44-59.

PART IV

Sample Approaches for Managing the
Organizational Reactions in Order to
Promote Worker Well-Being

7 Strategies for Managing Plant Closings and Downsizing

RICHARD H. PRICE

The current wave of economic change will produce both opportunities and challenges for human resource managers and other corporate decision makers. As companies adapt to changing markets they will be forced to close, relocate, or consolidate facilities. Ironically, while these closings are attempts to minimize costs and redeploy resources, they can be extremely costly in both financial and human terms. In the process of closing, relocation, or consolidation, decisions are made which can dramatically affect both the economic and psychological well-being of managers, workers, and community members. Managing the transitions associated with organizational decline and closings will become an even more critical role for human resource managers. It is not just the financial cost to a company of organizational closings that are at stake, but poorly managed transitions may carry with them the threat of regulatory legislation enacted in reaction to the human cost of poor management.

While it would appear that there are substantial incentives to minimize corporate costs by downsizing or closing a plant rapidly with as little communication as possible with workers, unions, and the community, this may be a costly strategy in the long run. Such strategies may bring unwanted legal sanctions on the corporation, prolong the costly payment of unemployment benefits, or incur a variety of other hidden costs that can and should be avoided.

On the other hand, there are strategies that human resource managers can employ to close a facility or reduce a work force that will minimize the costs to the corporation, to workers, and to the community at large. Managers have learned their skills for the most part in an era of economic growth. Few are trained or knowledgeable about the options

available for the management of organizational decline or retrenchment. And yet, management of decline is one of the major challenges
facing many managers today (Greenhalgh, 1982; Sutton, Eisenhardt, &
Jucker, 1986; Tomasko, 1987). In what follows, I will describe some
research documenting the human cost of unemployment, and recount a
case of a plant closing that illustrates how poor management produced
high costs to *both* workers and management. I will then examine a range
of layoff, redeployment, and employee enhancement strategies aimed
at minimizing the costs to both the corporation and workers and argue
that long-term adaptive capacities for the organization can be developed
through an orchestration of these strategies for the deployment of
human resources.

Plant Closings and Downsizing: The Impact

Research Evidence

While it has long been argued that involuntary unemployment has
significant physical and mental health effects on those who lose jobs
(Atkinson, Leim, & Leim, 1986; Catalano & Dooley, 1983; Cobb &
Kasl, 1977; Leim & Raymon, 1982), there has been a curious unwill-
ingness to acknowledge these impacts. This has been in part because of
scientific skepticism of evidence drawn from nonexperimental data. It
has also been because worker dislocation is frequently seen as merely
a "cost of doing business" to be passed on to the individual or government programs.

Recently, some of my colleagues (Kessler, Turner, & House, in press)
at the Michigan Prevention Research Center conducted a carefully
designed epidemiological survey of the impact of unemployment on
physical and mental health. To guard against selection effects that might
bias results by obtaining an unrepresentative sample of employed and
unemployed workers, the community survey obtained a representative
sample of 492 individuals. One third of them were currently unemployed, one third were previously unemployed, and one third had been
steadily employed. Respondents were interviewed twice over the course
of a year by professional interviewers using a face-to-face, 80-minute
interview. The interview protocol included questions about employment history, family information, assessments of financial hardship and
strain, and standard measures of physical and mental health with par-

ticular focus on anxiety, depression, suicide, drinking problems, and physical symptoms.

Results of this survey indicated significantly elevated measures of physical illness and depression. Indeed, these symptoms were severe enough to warrant treatment. Careful analyses of the data indicated that psychological symptoms were due primarily to increased levels of financial strain associated with job loss. The financial strain in turn produced major dislocations such as having to move, conflict within the family, and inability to get medical help, pay bills, or provide for one's family. A second intriguing finding was that being unemployed increased physical and mental health vulnerability to other life events such as an illness in the family or having to move.

In the past, such results have frequently been passed off as a product of faulty research designs. In this study, Kessler, Turner, and House not only guarded against this criticism by obtaining a representative community sample of employed and unemployed workers, they conducted further analyses that deserve attention. The question could be raised, for example, about whether those unemployed show physical and psychological symptoms because they are the people who remain unemployed after healthier workers have already become reemployed. That is, is the unemployed group under study biased by the fact that healthier workers have already found jobs? To guard against this bias, Kessler et al. combined the previously unemployed and employed groups in producing their estimates of the impact of unemployment. This is an extremely conservative test of the impact of unemployment, since it includes those persons previously unemployed who now have a job. Using this control their results still were strongly confirmed; physical and psychological symptoms remained high.

The second question a critic might ask is, are those who are now unemployed lacking jobs because they had symptoms before? That is, did their illness select them into unemployment status? To counter this criticism, Kessler et al. selected those currently and previously unemployed for whom the question of self-selection was extremely unlikely, those who were involuntarily unemployed as a consequence of layoffs and plant closings. Again, they found substantial impacts of unemployment. Stated in terms of relative risk, the unemployed groups compared with employed workers were between 1.5 and 3.5 times more likely to have severe symptoms. In validation studies, these scores are considered to be clinically significant and high enough to warrant professional intervention.

Thus the accumulated evidence and the research of Kessler et al. make it difficult to ignore evidence which is now nearly incontrovertible. The decision to subject others to involuntary unemployment, particularly those made vulnerable by virtue of other life circumstances, is a decision to inflict suffering on large segments of the work force. Shortly we will turn to the consideration of some of the alternatives to plant closings and mass unemployment, but first, let us consider the impact of a plant closing on a less scientific but perhaps more human scale.

Social scientists trained to be skeptical and yet appreciative of evidence gathered through careful research and analysis are inclined to be persuaded by the sort of evidence that Kessler, Turner, and House provide. To understand the impact of a plant closing on workers and families one needs to see the texture of everyday life as portrayed in works such as Slote (1969). In *Termination: The Closing at Baker Plant*, Al Slote describes a plant closing and its impact on the lives of not only the workers and their families, but on management as well. The author offers a similar story of a plant closing to tell, but one with perhaps yet another lesson, since the plant closing to be described had negative impacts not only on the workers and their families, but also on the corporation.

A Case Study: The Larck Closing

In the fall of 1981 a company that I shall call Larck Corporation, a large manufacturing company in the Midwest, discovered that its market had contracted and it had too much manufacturing capacity. Worldwide constrictions in its market made it clear that some form of downsizing had to be undertaken. Since Larck was a national corporation with a number of plants, a decision had to be made about which of their plants should be closed. A cost comparison at various plants indicated that at one of their plants—the Omega plant—the workers were considerably older. Indeed, over half the workers had 26 years in seniority, and company policy allowed retirement after 30 years of service. Further analysis indicated that the current contribution to pensions in their Omega plant was approximately $3.60 an hour, whereas in their Alpha plant their contribution was only $.60 an hour, and the average age of the worker was under 30.

From a purely financial standpoint, the company soon would be paying pensions to a large portion of their work force at Omega plant if it remained open. Closing it, on the other hand, would not only reduce manufacturing capacity, it would also mean that many of the workers at Omega plant would never reach 30 years of service and would not be entitled to full pension rights. The decision was predictable enough; Omega plant would be closed. Men, most of whom were between the ages of 50 and 60, and most of whom had been working as welders, would soon be without work and without the prospect of a pension, even though many were within two or three years of retirement.

The story takes an interesting turn at this point because some workers recognized that the plant closing decision appeared to be a clear case of age discrimination, and they sued Larck, Inc. A jury soon found that the evidence of age discrimination was compelling, that Larck had made its plant closing decision on the basis of the age of the work force. An ill-considered management decision produced a probably unnecessary loss for Larck, both financially and in terms of its reputation.

The law firm that had offered its services to the workers at Larck's Omega plant wanted to know what the plant closing had meant for the lives of the workers at Omega plant and asked me to interview the plaintiffs. It was agreed that the workers would be interviewed using the same research instrument that had earlier been used to do the epidemiological survey of unemployed workers, and that I would also find out additional information about their life circumstances.

My scientific curiosity was aroused because our research instrument and sampling frame, while producing reliable results, could not possibly capture the texture of the lives of our respondents in adequate detail. We agreed that I would interview each of the plaintiffs individually, but I was unprepared for what I then experienced. As we met for scheduled interviews I encountered men and their buddies, and husbands coming with their wives, to talk about what had happened to them.

My interviews using our standardized survey instrument confirmed what our larger, more representative, sample of unemployed workers had indicated. Many workers were experiencing severe symptoms of anxiety and depression; but it was hearing their stories in detail that revealed much more. Indeed, reflecting on those interviews nearly a year later and reviewing the interview protocols suggests at least eight themes that emerge from those interviews that add dimension and texture to our epidemiological findings. The following describes each of the eight themes that emerged and provides some examples in the words of these workers and their families.

A sense of betrayal and a feeling that an implicit contract had been violated. In interview after interview with these workers, a sense of outrage and betrayal emerged. Each of these workers and their families understood the company pension plan, whose rule was "30 and out." That is, they were entitled to a full pension after 30 years of service. As one worker said, "How could they work you up until the last few years and kick you out?" Still another worker who had worked as a pipe fitter and boiler maintenance person said

> I gave the best years of my life to Larck. I often didn't see my family at Christmas. There wasn't one holiday when I didn't have to go into work at least part of the time. I always wanted to work hard and protect my job, so we could have a good retirement. We used to work hard: I worked 19 days straight, had one day off, and then worked 14 days more. Once I worked five shifts in a row, and my family ended up not seeing me.

At this point, this worker's wife began to cry. These workers seemed to believe that loyalty and commitment should fulfill their side of an implicit social contract, and that the "30 and out" retirement would be the company's repayment for their loyalty and commitment.

A job search handicapped by age discrimination, poor health, and a bad economy. As these workers told their story of the job search that followed the plant closing, several themes emerged again and again that are especially salient in understanding the job search circumstances of older workers. Story after story emerged of a locally depressed economy in which few jobs were available. Interestingly, many of the workers interviewed reported that younger workers were being hired, but that when they themselves applied they were told that there were no openings.

One worker said, "I'd begun to chalk off the time until retirement period. Now I am 60 years old and no one will hire me." Another said, "It's like you're in a vacuum of hopelessness, like you go into a dream. I still dream about the shock. It comes back. It's like a death. At night I would get my work clothes out and lay them out. I'll be a basket case for two weeks just talking about this. I'm 58 years old, and who is going to hire me?" Another worker who had injured his back by engaging in heavy lifting in order to earn a piecework bonus said that as his unemployment continued, "I got scared. I am over 50, I had a back injury, who is going to hire me? Who would hire a man with a bad back at that age?"

Age discrimination during the job search was commonly reported. One worker who had a highly marketable work specialty as a pipe fitter reported that he felt he should have a reasonable chance of being reemployed. However, while potential employers would not mention it directly, they would not hire someone who was 55 years old.

A new job with low wages, little security, and no protective benefits. When some of these workers did, indeed, find employment, the jobs they found were of a far different kind than those they lost. Typically, they were part-time, low wage jobs with no health insurance or other protective benefits. These workers had rapidly begun to bump and slide down the economy.

In one interview, a worker reported he went into the army surplus business and was "not making it." Another reported that the only job he could find was as a part-time janitor at $3.75 an hour. Almost invariably, these workers deferred nonemergency medical care because they had no insurance and could not afford it. One worker, who was being treated for ulcers, said, "The doctor wants me to visit him every six months. I can't do it. It's $30 a visit."

Actual health problems or fear of them become a major source of uncertainty and distress. These older workers, for the most part, had reached an age where health problems were likely to increase. Lack of steady income or health insurance left them feeling fearful and uncertain about how they would cope with the financial problems associated with any deterioration in the health of a family member. A family who had a daughter living at home with a congenital heart defect expressed concern about this financial vulnerability. The wife stated, "I don't feel safe about retiring yet. One hospital stay could wipe a family out. Who would have thought I would be working still?"

Economic hardship forces other life change decisions that increase stress. Several workers reported that after depleting their life savings, they had to change their residence. In one case, a family moved to a southwestern state, where their mother had a small house. The labor market turned out to be even poorer there, and they were without plumbing or adequate heating in their new circumstances. A second example of economic hardship that forced other life transitions involved a worker's family who found themselves unable to make the payments on their house and were forced to move into a chicken coop. Still other examples of the ripple effect of economic hardship were reflected in the neglect of medical care which then exacerbated already existing health problems.

Family burden in multiple forms. The interviews revealed the impact of unemployment on families in a number of distinctively different forms. Among them were: (1) an increase in marital conflict and distress because of worry about unemployment and finances; (2) distress expressed by workers because they no longer felt that they could fulfill the role of provider; (3) children who were distressed because of changing life circumstances; (4) wives who experienced increases in workload burden or who were unable to relinquish them even though they themselves were not well; and (5) children who either had to defer further education or were not provided with material or health resources because of lack of finances.

One worker reported that his oldest son, who had a developmental disability, was upset at the prospect of moving to a chicken coop and refused to move. The worker felt upset by this but stated, "I had no choice. You never know whether you do right. It seems like everything's against you." A wife of a displaced worker reported that in the year following his job loss, the worker became extremely irritable and emotionally upset. Even though they had a strong marital relationship, she reported, "I wrote him a divorce letter. He was so irritable, I couldn't do anything right for him and the kids couldn't either." Another worker reported his distress at not being able to provide even small gifts for his grandchildren. "I have six or seven grandkids come at Christmas time. I can't do much at all for them. I used to belong to a Christmas club and save. Now I can't do anything. They're all disappointed and it makes you feel bad."

Continuing psychological distress, crisis, and vulnerability. One of the most striking aspects of the interviews was the sense of personal crisis, depression, and continuing anxiety provoked in workers and their families. At times the workers seemed almost embarrassed that so much powerful emotion was still being evoked.

The wife of one worker reported that six months after the plant closing, they were in a state of extreme crisis: "I cried and cried and couldn't believe it. I got so I couldn't even talk to neighbors or friends." This worker's wife reported that she had suicidal thoughts at that time, and during the summer and throughout the next winter there were occasions when neither of them went to bed for 24 hours at a time. "Why go to bed when there's nothing to get up for?" she asked. A number of workers reported that while they were ashamed of it, they still were unable to control their emotions. One said, "I couldn't believe it. It knocked the pegs out from under me. I never figured they would close the plant. I can't figure out why I can't control my emotions." While some workers appeared to have regained their psychological equilibrium, still others continued to display signs of chronic anxiety or depression and deep, uncontrollable emotions just below the surface. A number of interviews resulted in workers and their wives, to their embarrassment, bursting into tears.

Helplessness, uncertainty, and a fearful sense of the future. All of these workers were acutely aware that they were likely to live considerably longer, would have health and financial problems, and had little idea of how they would cope. As one worker's wife put it, "What we have lost wasn't a job, it was our whole future."

Another wife of a worker put it this way: "We decided to stick it out with Larck and were loyal to them. We didn't think they would ditch us and they did. It just keeps going on and on. It's always there [the feeling of insecurity]. I guess it is going to haunt us until the day we die." The wife of another worker said, "That was our whole plan: to work hard when we were young and do what we wanted to when we got older. We worked hard, but the other part didn't happen."

Of course, these are painful stories; the kind managers don't like to think about. What has just been described brings close to home the social and psychological fallout of the impact of a plant closing for workers and their families. In this case, not only did the workers become victims, but so did the corporation since a jury found it in violation of age discrimination laws. What are the alternatives? Does economic vitality depend on exacting large financial and personal costs on the lives of workers, and is the only recourse for those workers the protection of the law? There are alternatives to plant closings of the kind I have just described. In what follows, I will consider a range of options that may minimize the impact of organizational decline, both for workers and for the corporation.

Strategic Options for Coping with Organizational Decline

A Hierarchy of Organizational Strategies for Work Force Reduction

The most common organizational response to dealing with pressures for work force reduction has been to use layoffs as the primary strategy. While layoffs are the most typical strategy for work force reduction, Greenhalgh, Lawrence, and Sutton (1988) point out that there is actu-

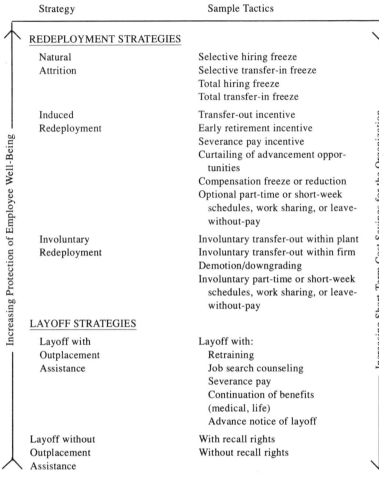

	Strategy	Sample Tactics
	REDEPLOYMENT STRATEGIES	
	Natural Attrition	Selective hiring freeze Selective transfer-in freeze Total hiring freeze Total transfer-in freeze
	Induced Redeployment	Transfer-out incentive Early retirement incentive Severance pay incentive Curtailing of advancement opportunities Compensation freeze or reduction Optional part-time or short-week schedules, work sharing, or leave-without-pay
	Involuntary Redeployment	Involuntary transfer-out within plant Involuntary transfer-out within firm Demotion/downgrading Involuntary part-time or short-week schedules, work sharing, or leave-without-pay
	LAYOFF STRATEGIES	
	Layoff with Outplacement Assistance	Layoff with: Retraining Job search counseling Severance pay Continuation of benefits (medical, life) Advance notice of layoff
	Layoff without Outplacement Assistance	With recall rights Without recall rights

Increasing Protection of Employee Well-Being

Increasing Short-Term Cost Savings for the Organization

Figure 7.1. Strategies and Tactics for Work Force Reduction: The Range of Options for Declining Organizations.

Source: Greenhalgh, Lawrence, & Sutton, 1988, p. 243.

ally a hierarchy of strategies for reducing the work force. This hierarchy is shown in Figure 7.1, which depicts five primary levels of strategies for work force reduction. It is also interesting to note that, as one goes up the hierarchy, there is a tradeoff between employee well-being and control over work continuity on the one hand and short-term cost savings to the organization on the other. Figure 7.1 also shows a number of different tactics that can be used to implement each of these broad strategies. Let us consider each of the strategies in turn.

Natural attrition. This strategy, of course, involves limiting the number of new employees joining a firm. Because other employees may retire or resign, the attrition strategy will provide a gradual decline in the work force. While it is the slowest strategy for work force reduction, attrition provides the most control for employees over the continuity of their work and is a strategy to which a number of U.S. firms, such as International Business Machines, maintain an active commitment.

Induced worker redeployment. Increasing incentives to transfer to undersupplied jobs by offering retraining or financial incentives can induce redeployment of the work force from overstaffed to understaffed segments of the company work force. Similarly, induced redeployment may mean producing inducements for leaving the organization such as financial incentives for early retirement. Job sharing or shortening work weeks or workdays is another tactic for inducing redeployment and will be discussed in more detail below.

Involuntary worker redeployment. This redeployment strategy differs from voluntary redeployment only in that employees are required to take other positions or accept reduced work hours or unpaid leaves. While this strategy is rapid in its effect on the work force, it also means that employee control over the continuity of employment is lost, even though employees will not lose their jobs under this strategy.

Layoffs with outplacement. Layoffs have the most rapid effect on short-term cost savings for a company, but layoff strategies have a major impact on employee control over their employment opportunities. Layoffs with placement counseling, as will be described below, provide a wider range of coping opportunities for laid-off workers; when a company supplies severance pay and health benefits, this option provides a reasonable latitude of options for laid-off workers.

Layoffs without outplacement. This strategy reduces employee control over worklife opportunities to a minimum, and produces, in some cases, the psychosocial effects described earlier in this chapter. While there is no question that layoffs without outplacement counseling services can produce higher short-term cost savings, in some cases this strategy may be shortsighted, and the long-term costs to the firm may be higher than anticipated.

This hierarchy of organizational strategies provides us with some perspective on the range of options open to managers faced with the painful dilemmas presented by the need to reduce the work force. In what follows, several of these strategies will be examined in more detail, focusing particularly on outplacement counseling and on job sharing as important tactics available when considering work force reduction.

The Role of Human Resource Managers

Managers face a number of dilemmas during the actual process of work force reduction, and it can be argued that communication with those leaving the organization and with remaining employees presents a series of challenges for which few managers are currently prepared.

Zammuto and Cameron (1985) have argued that today's managers are poorly educated to cope with the challenges of organizational decline. Corporate leaders in America have been taught that organizations must grow, and they frequently lack the experience, training, or knowledge that they need to manage an organization in decline. In fact, Sutton, Eisenhardt, and Jucker (1986) observe that managers are often forced to struggle with two competing tasks when they deal with declining organizations. On the one hand they must reduce the size of the work force, and on the other they must manage the remaining portion of the organization effectively.

Sutton, Eisenhardt, and Jucker (1986) have conducted a detailed series of interviews with employees in the Atari corporation to better understand the errors that are made in the context of managing organizational decline. Atari is an organization that had enjoyed enormous growth in the video game industry, but was suddenly faced with a rapid growth in competition, as well as a rapid decline in the demand for video games. Thus an organization that had been rapidly on the rise suddenly was faced with oceans of red ink, and the need to reduce the size of its work force.

Managers, or anybody for that matter, under stress experience a variety of cognitive and perceptual changes that actually reduce their ability to cope with the complex demands of stressful circumstances. In a now famous paper, Staw, Sandelands, and Dutton (1981) argue that when organizations, groups, or individual human beings are under stress, there is a tendency for them to stop carrying out more exploratory and less familiar responses, and to begin to rely on more well-rehearsed responses to a particular situation. They describe this as the *threat rigidity hypothesis*. They argue that threats increase the likelihood of rigid responses, which in many cases may be maladaptive, both for the individual and for organizations. Managers under siege may exhibit precisely these rigidities in the process of managing work force reduction.

Sutton, Eisenhardt, and Jucker (1986) tell the story of a management of work force reduction at Atari corporation, and in the process identify a number of managerial dilemmas and tactics to cope with them that are worth reviewing in some detail. Six of them will be considered here.

Examine layoff policies for evenhandedness. There is considerable research to indicate that when organizations are forced to shrink their work force, the managerial segment of the work force is reduced more slowly than is the bottom segment of the organizational hierarchy. In Atari's case, Sutton and his colleagues observed that Atari had hired excessive numbers of managers during the great growth in sales that Atari had experienced, and its top-heavy structure created a number of problems during downsizing. Retaining expensive managers who had little work to do drained financial resources from other parts of the company which would have helped the company to recover. In addition, keeping upper level employees who had little to do sent a symbolic message to lower level employees who remained, and morale was severely damaged. Furthermore, middle level managers who had little to do spent most of their time engaging in company politics and spreading rumors about what would happen next during the work force reduction.

If employees must leave, allow them to leave with dignity. During the Atari layoffs, Sutton and his colleagues indicate that Atari employees were often given their notice and summarily escorted off the premises by security guards after their badges had been collected and they had been told that they were laid off as of that moment. Interestingly, these humiliating practices resulted in former Atari employees filing a class action suit against Atari. Sutton et al. also observed that these humiliating practices had negative impacts on the surviving employees, who lost their respect and trust of Atari managers. In addition, newspaper stories soon began to characterize Atari corporation layoff strategies as haphazard and cruel, thus hurting Atari's ability to recruit future employees.

Help those laid off to find new jobs. Atari provided reasonably good severance pay for its employees, but little effort was made to find new

jobs for displaced workers. In fact, layoff efforts were so haphazard that
some employees were rehired only a week after they had been laid off,
resulting in a one-week vacation for the employees at approximately
eight times their usual pay. Sutton et al. also emphasized that those
within the company who remained noted Atari's lack of effort to find
new jobs for displaced workers, lost trust in the company, and were
more disposed to leave at the earliest opportunity.

Avoid belittling those who have been displaced. In Atari's case, some
managers felt that they could boost morale within the company by
communicating the idea that the weakest workers, who they called the
"dead wood" or the "rotten apples" had been laid off, thus leaving the
work force "lean and mean." Unfortunately, this strategy backfired in
a number of ways. Top management credibility was undermined among
the survivors, who knew that displaced workers were not less able. Still
others doubted management's ability and assumed that Atari had been
inept in hiring such people in the first place.

Keep employees informed. During a period of organizational decline, uncertainty is experienced as threatening, while during periods
of organizational growth, uncertainty is seen as exciting and challenging. During decline, managers are unlikely to communicate much about
the future of the company, partly because they are uncertain about what
the future actually holds, and partly because they fear the development
of rumors. Ironically, rumors will always develop to fill in the vacuum
of information that exists. In the case of Atari, the uncertainty that
existed was fed by long periods of managerial silence. This meant that
organizational effectiveness and work efficiency declined as employees
compared various rumors of what might happen next. Sutton et al. argue
that employees should be kept fully informed of various developments
and should even oversupply, rather than undersupply, information. They
observe that some declining organizations install hot lines so that
employees can get the latest information and find out about the validity
of various rumors. Mass meetings and other communication strategies
are also recommended.

Set realistic expectations. One of the great dilemmas experienced by
managers during a period of layoff and decline has to do with the
question of whether it is more appropriate to give employees hope, thus
motivating them to redouble their effort, or to take it away, so as not to
set unrealistic expectations. The danger of offering false hope, of
course, is that trust is lost when unrealistic expectations turn out to be
unfulfilled. Sutton and his colleagues argue for realistic and even

slightly pessimistic predictions in the context of organizational decline, both because it helps employees plan for their own future and because it engenders trust rather than mistrust in the long run.

Proactive Steps for Managers

Price and D'Aunno (1984) have argued that human resource managers in a plant closing or work force reduction are in a critical position that can help reduce costs, both for laid-off workers and for corporate management. A key insight, Price and D'Aunno argue, is the recognition that the corporation is to a certain extent dependent on the workers to find reemployment as rapidly as possible, because the corporate costs of unemployment benefits will decrease substantially if workers are reemployed rapidly. In addition, of course, human resource managers can help their corporations avoid additional costs that local communities may exact in reaction to thoughtlessly and poorly planned plant closings. These include community sanctions such as reductions in tax shelters for corporations, boycotts and poor sales, inadequate police protection, and tarnished public images.

Taber, Walsh, and Cooke (1978) have argued that while a variety of health and human service agencies exist in most communities, they are frequently not well coordinated, and often are not by themselves equipped to respond quickly to the needs of workers unemployed by plant closings. At the same time, workers may not have information about possible service agencies and in so doing contribute to the problem. Buss and Redburn (1981) suggest two tactics to overcome these problems. First, the human resource managers can make information on workers whose jobs will be terminated available to local human service agencies. They can also allow representatives of various service agencies inside the plant prior to layoffs to provide workers with information about available services. An additional strategy suggested by Buss and Redburn is for the human resource managers to develop ties with economic development agencies in the community. Local planning agencies, particularly those associated with employment and training, can identify new training and employment opportunities for laid-off workers.

The benefits of these strategies include the improvement of public relations, reducing the risk of legal and economic sanctions against the corporation, and rapid re-employment of workers where possible, to reduce capital expenditures for unemployment benefits. Price and

D'Aunno (1984) argue that plant closings and downsizing do not inevitably imply that corporations must "win" at the expense of workers and their communities. Human resource managers can arrange programs that provide mutual benefit for workers and the company, programs that can reduce human and material costs for both corporate actors and for laid-off workers.

Reemployment Assistance: Reducing Corporate Liability and Enhancing Worker Well-Being

While plant closings and other forms of downsizing are designed to reduce costs or reposition capital, they can be extremely expensive. This critical insight is frequently missed by managers and corporate decision makers. Furthermore, corporate decision makers and managers frequently fail to recognize that they actually depend on the behavior of workers and unions during and after a plant closing to reduce corporate costs. Benefits provided to displaced workers are often more expensive if workers are not rapidly reemployed. Thus, the more rapidly workers are reemployed, the less cost to the corporation. Indeed, corporate profits depend on the reemployment success of displaced workers.

Furthermore, Gordus, Jarley, and Ferman (1981) report that in recent years unions have used lawsuits as a way of attempting to improve the terms of settlements associated with plant closings. In cases where companies have made systematic and visible efforts to aid worker reemployment, the chances of such lawsuits will be lower. It follows that human resource managers who develop reemployment assistance programs should reduce the costs for management in unemployment benefits and also reduce the chances of lawsuits by workers.

A program to aid in job seeking. Entering the work force for the first time, or reentering it after a period of unemployment, represents a major social transition. Caplan, Vinokur, Price, and van Ryn (in press) have developed an intervention program to aid unemployed persons in their job searches and to help them sustain their efforts in the face of inevitable setbacks. The program also has been rigorously evaluated in the context of a randomized field experiment.

Participants were recruited from unemployment lines. Program trainers established trust between the participants and the trainers before introducing other agenda items that were part of the training. Trust was established by having trainers engage in self-disclosure by describing a previous period of their own unemployment, their feelings during it, and ultimately their success in obtaining a new job. The trainers' expertise or "expert power" was also established by describing the training program in detail and showing how it was based on behavioral science research. Once the preconditions of trust and expertise had been established, the unemployed participants were more receptive to the training program itself and to the trainers' efforts to help in job searches.

It was assumed that both skill in job-seeking activities *and* the motivation to carry them out were critical ingredients in enhancing effective job-seeking behavior. The program taught participants a variety of skills, including identifying jobs which required the experience, skills, and background of the participants; effectively searching one's social network for job leads; and self-presentation skills, both in presenting résumés and in job interviews.

In addition to the skill component, the program was aimed at enhancing motivation to continue job-seeking, even in the face of fear of rejection or actual rejections by prospective employers. The training program helped participants to see that rejections were an inevitable part of the job search process, to normalize this event, and to treat it as a commonplace aspect of the job search activity. At the same time, motivating job search skills were taught through processes of graded exposure where trainers reinforced and applauded new achievements, as did other trainees in supporting each others' efforts.

The program was also aimed at inoculating participants against setbacks in their job searches. This was accomplished by having participants anticipate situations in which setbacks were likely, generating alternative methods for overcoming the dysfunctional responses to setbacks, and acquiring skills needed to cope more effectively with temporary reversals. Finally, the intervention was designed to increase social support for participants, both from trainers and from peers in the program.

This program, aimed at the life transition of reentry into the labor market, was evaluated in a randomized field experiment involving 928 participants (Caplan, Vinokur, Price, & van Ryn, in press). The results of the experiment indicated that those who participated in the program obtained jobs of higher quality in terms of earnings and job satisfaction. Even among those who were not reemployed as rapidly, higher motivation to continue seeking work was observed. There was also some evidence that the intervention alleviated some of the negative mental health consequences of job loss.

Work Sharing: The Redeployment of Worker Resources

Work sharing represents still another way to reduce the work force without eliminating jobs. In some cases, this strategy can have a number of additional benefits as well. When McCarthy and Rosenberg (1981) conducted a study of work-sharing plans among 36 companies in private sector service and manufacturing companies as well as public agencies, both unionized and nonunionized, the employers gave the following reasons for developing work-sharing plans. Work sharing provides: (1) an alternative to layoffs; (2) the capacity to adjust to skill shortages; (3) the ability to retain valuable and skilled workers; (4) the ability to achieve/maintain production flexibility; (5) the possibility to advance affirmative action goals; (6) improvement in efficiency and organizational performance; and (7) an opportunity to prepare employees for retirement.

As an alternative to layoffs and plant closings, work-sharing programs can be defined as reduced work hour approaches that have the effect of sharing the available work among a greater number of people. McCarthy and Rosenberg (1981) argue that many groups in society are actively seeking flexible solutions to a changing work environment, and that work sharing is a viable alternative for some employers. They suggest that work-sharing programs fall into three general categories: (1) temporary reduction in work hours; (2) permanent reduction in work hours; and (3) flexible worklife options.

Temporary reductions in work hours can take several forms and are typically adopted for a limited time during an economic downturn. They may involve a shortened workweek in which all employees in the affected work groups work fewer hours and receive less pay. Another form of temporary reduction in hours is the rotation layoff, where all affected employees rotate weeks of work and weeks of nonwork. A third form is the shared-work unemployment compensation program. This is an experimental program operating in California that enables workers to be partially compensated through state unemployment insurance for temporarily shortened work weeks.

Another work sharing alternative is *permanent reduction in work hours*. These programs tend to be institutionalized in collective bargaining agreements or personnel policies and most typically are initiated in response to employee desires for shorter work hours. These programs include extended holidays and vacations or a part-time voluntary reduction in total work hours, accompanied by salary reductions and prorated fringe benefits, or shorter workweeks established on a permanent basis.

Finally, among work-sharing strategies a range of *flexible worklife options* that provide periodic breaks in work lives of full-time employees are available. These include phased retirement of a gradual, flexible, or transitional kind; leaves, including social service leaves; sabbaticals; and voluntary time/income tradeoff arrangements. In these arrangements, employees voluntarily reduce their wages or salary in exchange for additional time off work.

McCarthy and Rosenberg (1981) indicate that companies that have successfully developed work-sharing arrangements typically have very specific goals in mind and solicit ideas about the structure and purpose of programs from employees, union officials, and management. They also have an orientation that allows experimentation and takes a "let's try it and see if it works" attitude that allows feedback on the benefits and shortcomings of programs. Typically, successful programs are implemented on a small scale and expanded where they are successful.

Two kinds of businesses tend to be most typically involved in work-sharing programs. One type is young, high-pressure, fast-paced, often high-technology firms, where innovation is a general style and special skills are highly valued. Work sharing allows companies to retain valued workers even in a downturn. The second type of organization tends to be family-oriented businesses that exhibit a special concern about the needs of their employees.

Like all patterns of organizational adaptation, work-sharing arrangements can have real advantages for both workers and for companies under special circumstances, but may have some costs as well. The costs may include an increase in administrative activities to assure coverage and scheduling, such as additional paperwork and more supervision.

McCarthy and Rosenberg (1981) observe that in the future, human resource development will become increasingly integrated with corporate planning and must be oriented to the organizations' top management goals. Human resource managers who recognize the multiple goals and needs of workers and build flexibility into management practices will be more likely to produce successes for their companies, both in periods of growth and decline.

Options for an aging work force. Older workers present special dilemmas and challenges when work force reduction is a possibility. And, of course, the demographics of the work force are changing. As the baby boom ages, and workers from the period of low birth rates enter the work force, the average age of workers will climb from 36 years of age today to 39 by the year 2000. Older workers tend to be more stable, experienced, and reliable, but they also may bring with them less willingness to relocate, change occupations, or undertake retraining. In the last quarter-century, the proportion of persons over 65 in the U.S. population has increased from 9.2% to 11.8% and is expected to continue rising. Furthermore, people are retiring earlier and living longer. The median retirement age is now 62, and life expectancy since the 1950s for 60-year-olds has increased from 77 to 80.

Kraut (1987) has reported on a recent study of retirees that surveyed more than 10,000 retirees from a large electronics company. Survey respondents included workers at all levels, from assembly line to engineers and accountants, managers and executives. When retirees were asked if they would be willing to come back to the company on a supplemental basis to work as temporary employees, 68% said they would be interested in returning. Willingness to return seemed tied to the recency of retirement, with the highest proportion of people stating a willingness to return from those most recently retired. The primary interest expressed was in part-time work rather than full-time work. Most typically, respondents stated that they were interested in working a few days a week; a smaller percentage reported an interest in working a few hours a day.

Kraut (1987) notes that a new adaptability on the part of industry to accommodate the desire of experienced workers for part-time work could provide the industry with greater flexibility. Retired workers can serve as a buffer to deal with short-term peaks in the workload, and during economic downturns, when retired workers would be used less, they could protect the long-term employment security of younger full-time workers. Retirees typically are experienced, trained, and generally loyal to the company for whom they worked, and their vigor can be maintained by a shorter work schedule. Kraut suggests that scheduling and administrative complexities will exist with this strategy, but an experiment in a two-county area surrounding a major plant produced successful results for the electronics firm.

Malcolm Morrison (1986) has challenged our well-institutionalized concept of retirement, and describes a number of alternative work forms for older workers that may provide options for better educated and healthier older persons and for society in general. Among the options he describes are phased retirement, generally designed to permit job retention with reduced work schedules, a prorated salary, and promoted benefits.

Another option described by Morrison (1986) is that of annuitant pools. This strategy involves the employment of the company's own retirees, also described by Kraut (1987). Full retirement benefits usually continue, and annuitant pools can involve temporary, full-time, or part-time assignments and restructuring of jobs. Wages are monitored so as not to exceed Social Security's earning test limitations. An additional option for retired workers is contract work, in which older persons work as independent contractors on a fee-for-service basis. These arrangements frequently occur in personal services industries, technical consulting, sales, and similar fields.

Morrison (1986) also observes that job redesign and multiple flexible work arrangements for older workers are especially effective when experienced employees have long-standing clients, as often happens in the financial, insurance, or real estate industries. While such arrangements are not offered specifically for older workers, they tend to be used most by older workers.

All of these options imply a different view of worklife and retirement than currently exists for older workers. Instead of continuous upward mobility, employers and workers might view such policies as horizontal job mobility, reduced responsibility and income, and gradual diminution of responsibility and reward as a typical pattern for older workers. Morrison believes these options will be feasible only when the social values that now emphasize progressively upward mobility can be modified to reflect a continuum of worklife, encompassing upward, horizontal, and downward mobility.

Retraining: Enhancing Organizational Adaptability for Future Turbulence

Obviously, work force reduction is a short-term solution for American industry. Business cycles will certainly produce the need for work force reduction in the future as they have in the past. But ultimately our ability to be competitive will not be based on short-term work force reduction but on more adaptable organizational strategies and more skillful and adaptive workers. Training to prevent worker obsolescence is a key approach in any long-term strategy to enhance organizational effectiveness. Technological change to increase competitiveness carries with it its own demands for a work force capable of responding to the competition. Gordus, Jarley, and Ferman (1981) report that their survey of employers indicated that employers felt they needed people who had skills such as adequate communication and computational skills, the ability to follow directions, and the ability to confront a situation, analyze it, and choose among the options available for resolving problems.

Since the Industrial Revolution, increasing mechanization has been a prominent feature of the work force. Today, however, a major transformation is occurring in manufacturing. Computer-based technologies may fundamentally alter not only the service industries, but basic manufacturing as well. Technological change is also affecting health care industries, insurance, banking, auto manufacturing, and still other sectors.

Despite these challenges, systematically developed programs for retraining the work force and preventing worker obsolescence are relatively unusual. Gordus, Gohrband, and Meiland (1987) have reported a series of case studies of corporations that have implemented such programs, either jointly with unions or unilaterally. An excellent example is the Polaroid corporation's program in Cambridge, Massachusetts. Polaroids' Fundamental Skills Program has become a critical part of their system of employee compensation and promotion. Gordus et al. report the program has demonstrated a capacity to assess and certify the skills of employees who have gone through their training and assessment sequence. The program is organized around a system of carefully designed referrals, individual consulting, and personal assessment conducted by Polaroid's human resources development group.

The Polaroid effort is aimed at focusing on skills people need to improve their job performance and prepare for job growth. Each employee is counseled confidentially by a member of the human resources development group, assessment tests are conducted, and the results of those tests can be used as credentials for qualifying for a more desirable job. In the Polaroid program, participation is voluntary, but employees recognize that improved employee skill is a major route to promotion in the company.

Gordus, Gohrband, and Meiland (1987) mention a number of critical program elements to be included in a program for preventing skills obsolescence. They include:

- a counseling and educational guidance component that helps employees decide what kind of training they may take.
- an assessment system that allows the pinpointing of areas where training is needed.
- a support system, including tuition assistance, time off from work, and recognition among managers of the achievements resulting from continued education.
- a differentiated program focusing on basic skills, vocational skills, and general communication and organizational skills.
- a management development component to enhance management skills.

Currently management training is widely accepted but worker training is much less the norm. However, as fewer young workers enter the work force in the future and new demands for adaptability increase, businesses that compete successfully will be more likely to invest in continuous programs of training to prevent worker obsolescence.

Conclusion

There is little doubt that economic turbulence, mergers, technological changes, and other attempts to increase competitiveness will continue to stimulate organizational efforts to reduce the size of the work force. Many of these efforts will be unnecessarily costly both in terms of financial loss and in terms of well-being for both corporations and workers. However, a range of strategies exists for work force reduction that are underused and can aid organizational adaptability while maintaining a reasonable level of worker well-being. Among the strategies discussed in this chapter are the use of natural attrition, induced and voluntary redeployment of workers, and least desirable but sometimes necessary layoffs with outplacement.

However, managers have been trained to manage organizational growth, and few have been trained or have thought much about managing organizational decline. Deliberate downsizing and decline has to be managed while at the same time trying to maintain an effective organization. Few managers are able to do this well. Nevertheless, we are beginning to learn lessons about how to manage decline that may allow us to avoid some of the hidden and unanticipated costs to the company and unnecessary cruelty to workers. There are a number of proactive steps that managers can take in the face of organizational decline. They include programs for reemployment assistance and work sharing. The most future-oriented and preventive strategy for both the organization and the individual is retraining to prevent worker obsolescence. These human resource strategies will be adopted by companies for tough-minded rather than tender-hearted reasons. They are part of the key to long-term organizational adaptation and competitiveness.

References

Atkinson, T., Liem, R., & Liem, J. H. (1986). The social costs of unemployment: Implications for social support. *Journal of Health and Social Behavior, 27*, 317-331.

Buss, T. F., & Redburn, F. S. (1981, May). How to shut down a plant. *Industrial Management*, pp. 4-9.

Caplan, R. D., Vinokur, A. D., Price, R. H., & van Ryn, M. (in press). Job seeking, reemployment and mental health: A randomized field experiment in coping with job loss. *Journal of Applied Psychology*.

Catalano, R., & Dooley, D. (1983). Health effects and economic instability: A test of economic stress hypothesis. *Journal of Health and Social Behavior, 27*, 277-287.

Cobb, S., & Kasl, S. V. (1977). *Termination: The consequences of job loss.* The U.S. Government Printing Office, DHEW (NIOSH) No. 77-224.

Gordus, J. P., Jarley, P., & Ferman, L.A. (1981). *Plant closings and economic dislocation.* Kalamazoo, MI: W. E. Upjohn Institute for Employment Research.

Gordus, J., Gohrband, C., & Meiland, R. (1987). Information Series #322, Eric Clearinghouse on Adult Career and Vocational Education. Columbus: Ohio State University.

Greenhalgh, L. (1982). Maintaining organizational effectiveness during organizational retrenchment. *Journal of Applied Behavioral Science, 19*, 155-170.

Greenhalgh, L., Lawrence, A. T., & Sutton, R. I. (1988). Determinants of work force reduction strategies in declining organizations. *Academy of Management Review, 13*, 241-254.

Kessler, R. C., Turner, J. B., & House, J. S. (in press). The effects of unemployment on health in a community survey: Main, modifying, and mediating effects. *Journal of Social Issues*.

Kraut, A. I. (1987). Retiree: A new resource for American industries. *Personnel Administration, 32*(8).

Leim, R., & Raymon, P. (1982). Health and social costs of unemployment. *American Psychologist, 37*, pp. 1116-1124.

McCarthy, M., & Rosenberg, G. (1981). *Work sharing: Case studies.* Kalamazoo, MI: W.E. Upjohn Institute for Employment Research.

Morrison, M. (1986, Winter). Work and retirement in an aging society. *Daedalus, Journal of the American Academy of Arts and Sciences*, pp. 269-294.

Price, R. H., & D'Aunno, T. (1983). Managing work force reduction. *Human Resource Management, 22*(4), 413-430.

Slote, A. (1969). *Termination: The closing at Baker plant*. Indianapolis, IN: Bobbs-Merrill.

Staw, B. M., Sandelands, L. E., & Dutton, J. E. (1981). Threat-rigidity effects in organizational behavior: A multi-level analysis. *Administrative Science Quarterly, 26*, 501-524.

Sutton, R. I., Eisenhardt, K. M., & Jucker, J. V. (1986). Managing organizational decline: Lessons from Atari. *Organizational Dynamics, 14*(2), 17-29.

Taber, T. D., Walsh, J. T., & Cooke, R. A. (1978). Developing a community-based program for reducing the social impact of a plant closing. *Journal of Applied Behavioral Science*, pp. 133-155.

Tomasko, R. M. (1987). *Downsizing: Reshaping the corporation of the future*. New York: American Management Association.

Zammuto, R. F. & Cameron, K. S. (1985). Environmental decline and organizational response. In L. L. Cummings & B. M. Staw (Eds.), *Research in organizational behavior, 7* (pp. 223-262). Greenwich, CT: JAI Press.

8 Strategies for Integrating the Family Needs of Workers into Human Resource Planning

ELLEN GALINSKY

An Emphasis on Preschool Education

In a nationwide speaking tour for the Committee for Economic Development, Owen Butler, the former chairman of Procter and Gamble, is fond of quoting his predecessor who used to say that if he had to get rid of all the people in his company but was left with his plants, his equipment, and technology, he would be unable to rebuild his business in five years. If, on the other hand, he could keep the employees but was stripped of his plants, equipment, and technology, in the very same time period he could refashion his company to be as competitive as ever.

The point that Owen Butler makes is not an uncommon one these days: An investment in human capital makes better business sense than an investment in capital equipment and is absolutely necessary in a time of severe competitive pressure from a global economy. As the editors of *Business Week* magazine stated recently, "The nation's ability to compete is threatened by inadequate investment in our most important resource—people" ("Human Capital," 1988).

Both the editors of *Business Week* and the Committee for Economic Development take this point one step further to what is perhaps a surprising conclusion. The *Business Week* story asserts that "as the economy comes to depend more and more on women and minorities, we face a massive job of educating and training—starting before kindergarten. Can we afford it? We have no choice" ("Human Capital, 1988").

A report entitled *Children in Need* prepared by the Committee for Economic Development (1987) also called for quality preschool programs for all disadvantaged three- and four-year olds. They stated:

152

Quality education for *all children* is not an expense; it is an investment. Failure to educate is the true expense. In addition to improving our schools, investing in the careful nurturing of children from before birth through age five will deliver a handsome profit to society and to the individuals and families who have so much to gain. (p. 2)

It is not surprising to hear claims for preschool programs from educators and public policy makers today. After all, over a decade of research has revealed that comprehensive early childhood programs are cost-effective because they reduce the likelihood that poor children will be swept into a path of school and life failure (Berruta-Clement, Schweinhart, Barnett, Epstein, & Weikart, 1984; Lally, Mangione, & Honig, 1987). The Select Committee on Children, Youth, and Families in the House of Representatives (1984) has affixed a price tag to such an investment: a dollar spent in early childhood education saves $4.75 in reduced expenditures for remedial education, welfare, and juvenile justice.

The business community, on the other hand, has rarely, if ever, paid attention to early education. Their interest when focused on schooling, has been directed at secondary or higher education. Thus, one must ask: What is behind these somewhat surprising recommendations that early education is a key to business competitiveness?

The answer to that question resides in economic factors. Because we are facing a labor shortage due to a drop in the population growth—from 1.9% per year in the 1950s to .07% per year by 2000 (Johnston, 1987)—for the sake of the economy we as a country can no longer afford to ignore the reality that one in four children does not complete high school (U.S. Department of Education, 1988), and that 15% of recent graduates of urban high schools read at less than sixth grade level (Kozol, 1985). In fact, in some parts of the country the labor shortage is already being felt. Unemployment may be as low as 2%, and employers do not have their pick of an endless stream of baby boomers. Furthermore, some are having trouble finding employees skilled enough for the changing information-based economy and even competent enough to be trained. According to Jonathan Kozol, of 8 million unemployed adults, 4 to 6 million lack the skills to be retrained for high-tech jobs (Kozol, 1985).

Thus today's competitive business interests have the potential for enhancing the well-being of families. If society takes greater responsibility for providing good quality programming for children, their positive development could be enhanced and presumably family stress could be reduced. But will we take that route? An examination of the various early childhood initiatives that have been stimulated by these demographic realities reveals that there are several directions that may be taken, some with negative repercussions.

Potential Pitfalls

Concentrating on Schooling and Ignoring the Child Care Needs of Employed Parents

In numerous states there has been increased interest in providing preschool programs within the public schools. In New York, for example, the Commissioner's Task Force on Children and Youth At Risk (1988) recommends that the Commissioner of Education, the Board of Regents, and the State Education Department "initiate developmentally appropriate early childhood education programs for all children starting in communities with the highest concentrations of disadvantaged families" (p. 7).

The problems with developing preschool programs within the schools is that they are part-day programs. A recent nationwide survey conducted by Bank Street College and Wellesley College (Mitchell, 1988) found that 80% of preschool programs within the public school operate only during the school year and 60% of them offer a daily session of three hours or less. Furthermore, 90% of superintendents said that they did not plan to increase the hours of operation in the near future. This policy strategy runs counter to what has been labelled a "revolution" (Smith, 1979)—the large increase in the number of employed mothers. In 1987, 57% of the mothers of preschool children were in the labor force, up from 39% in 1985 (U.S. Department of Commerce, Bureau of the Census, 1987). Hofferth and Phillips (1987) predict a continued influx. By the mid-1990s, they estimate, two thirds of preschool children will have mothers in the labor force.

Thus it stands to reason that part-day programs within the public schools, while potentially good for children, might have a negative impact on employed parents. Parents who enroll their young child in public-school preschool programs would have to make other arrangements for that child before and after school. Since the supply of before- and after-school programs in no way meets the current demand (U.S.

Department of Labor, 1988), many parents might be forced into make-shift arrangements. Not only might the daily schedule cause conflict for the parent, so would the yearly schedule: vacations, holidays, closings for teachers' conferences, and snow days.

The research projects that I have been directing over the past decade at Bank Street College reveal that such child care problems already take a heavy toll on employed parents. We have found that parents are currently putting together patchwork arrangements that frequently fall apart. For example, a survey of 931 employed parents in three corporations conducted by Resources for Child Care Management (RCCM) and Bank Street College indicated that the families have as many as three to four different child care arrangements (Lurie, Galinsky, & Hughes, 1988). Furthermore, we and others have found that there is a significant relationship between the number of child care arrangements that parents use and the number of times that these arrangements fall apart (Shinn, Ortiz-Torres, Morris, Simko, & Wong, 1987; Hughes, 1987; Galinsky, 1988a). We found that 63% of the employees had at least one breakdown of their usual child care arrangement within the past three months, and 22% had three or more breakdowns.

In assessing all of the potential predictors of psychological adjustment at home or on the job, we have found that the breakdown of child care arrangements ranks as one of the most significant. In the nationally representative study we conducted for *Fortune* magazine of 405 employed mothers and fathers (Galinsky & Hughes, 1987), the breakdown of child care arrangements was linked to higher levels of stress. Only 17% of the parents with no breakdown in their child care arrangements reported feeling nervous or stressed "often" or "very often" in the past three months, as compared to 33% of those who experienced more numerous breakdowns.

The breakdown of child care arrangements may even have physical repercussions. In the *Fortune* study we found that child care breakdown was significantly associated with more stress-related health problems.

Even more profound is the fact that child care breakdown may impact the marital relationship. In Bank Street's study at Merck and Co., Inc., a pharmaceutical company (Hughes & Galinsky,1987), we assessed the respondents' overall satisfaction with their marriages, as well as marital companionship (the extent to which the relationships were caring and supportive), and marital tension (the extent to which the couples disagreed) and found that employees who experienced more frequent breakdowns in their child care arrangements were less satisfied with their marriages and reported less companionship and more tension in these relationships.

Finally, child care breakdown also may permeate one's satisfaction as a parent. The Bank Street Merck study found that employees who experienced more breakdowns in their child care were less satisfied in their role as parents.

Thus if the response to the increased competitive pressure of the global economy is to provide more part-day preschool programs within the public schools, employed parents' well-being may be adversely affected. Perhaps even more ironically, the current productivity of employed parents may also be jeopardized. We and others have found that more numerous child care arrangements and thus more frequent breakdowns are linked to higher levels of absenteeism and more tardiness. In addition, child care breakdown can have a negative impact on employees' ability to concentrate on the job (Galinsky & Hughes, 1987; Galinsky, 1988a).

Accordingly, several of the major federal legislative initiatives proposed in the 100th Congress focus on expanding part-day preschool programs to full-day working day coverage. This is one of the provisions of the Act for Better Child Care Services (ABC) introduced by Senators Dodd and Cranston and by Representatives Kildee, Snowe, and Hawkins. It is also the rationale of a bill entitled Smart Start introduced by Senator Kennedy. This bill would concentrate on four-year-olds, creating new programs and expanding part-day programs (such as Head Start and Pre-K programs within the public schools) so they would provide full working day coverage.

Concentrating on Increasing the Supply of Programs While Giving Less Attention to Program Quality

It is interesting that the current widespread interest in the early years has largely grown out of two notions: (1) the productivity of our current work force is affected by the stability of the child care system; and (2) the productivity of our future work force will be affected by the early education children receive. These tenets presuppose that care and education are separate for the young child. However, if one takes a developmental viewpoint, it becomes apparent that young children need care in order to learn and are, in fact, learning in whatever setting we as adults place them, whether such settings are labelled "child care" or "school." It is the quality, not the name of the program, that makes a difference.

It has been one of my frustrations in dealing with policy makers and serving on task forces over the past several years that the debate on the early years tends to filter down into discussions of increasing the supply of programs or giving money to parents to pay for programs. A subsidy for parents is the "child care" proposal of President Bush. In one state task force on work and family, the words "quality," "affordable," and "available" were used throughout the drafts of the report. However, numerous requests on the part of task force members, myself included, to recommend initiatives to improve quality never seemed to make their way into the final report written by the Governor's staff. The report instead concentrated on increasing the supply of child care. However, if one wants preschool programs to increase the competence of our future work force, then the type of program clearly makes a difference.

The current attempts to improve quality, moreover, reveal two different trends. One path is based on the assumption that young children need more of an emphasis on skills, the back-to-basics thrust that has been advocated by school boards, superintendents, and parents. They call for more reading, writing, and math earlier, stressing the academic preparation necessary to prepare young children for elementary school.

The other path has been forged by some organizations within the early childhood and elementary school fields. In November 1986, the National Association for the Education of Young Children (NAEYC), the largest professional association of early childhood educators with over 60,000 members, and the National Association for Elementary School Principals (NAESP) held a joint news conference decrying the push to pressure young children in developmentally inappropriate ways. David Elkind, then President of NAEYC, warned that if early educational programs were not mindful of how young children learn (through direct experience and play rather than paper and pencil tasks or drill and practice), the emphasis on early education might not produce the desired results. Samuel Sava, the President of NAESP, concurred, citing teachers' reports that young children in pressure-cooker learning environments in the preschool years seemed to be burning out, turning off to learning in the elementary school years.

It is important to remember that the research cited as demonstrating the benefits of early education was conducted in exemplary sites, such as the High/Scope program in Ypsilanti, Michigan (Berruta-Clement et al., 1984). These programs were developmentally appropriate, based on a rich experiential curriculum. The children did not sit at desks, and did not do worksheets—they used materials, took trips, and dictated stories. Fortunately, the words "developmentally appropriate" are being used in policy recommendations such as Senator Kennedy's Smart Start legislation and the final report of the New York State Education Department Commissioner's Task Force on the Education of Children and Youth at Risk. It will be extremely important to carry through, however, so that this concept is translated into program practice if we want to educate young children well.

Ignoring the Staffing Crisis

Some of the recent efforts to provide early childhood programs, particularly within child care settings, also ignored one of the most central aspects of quality—the high turnover of staff. Child care providers have the second highest turnover rate of any profession—42% leave the field annually. This turnover has been linked to low salaries. Seventy percent of child care workers earn less than poverty level wages (Whitebook, Pemberton, Lombardi, Galinsky, Bellm, & Fillinger, 1988). It is obvious that the best physical settings and curriculum materials are worth very little if staff change is constant. Research has begun to reveal that a revolving-door series of child care providers has a negative effect on children's development (Cummings, 1986; Howes, 1988). Thus efforts to provide quality early childhood programs must include strategies to address high staff turnover.

Not Providing Comprehensive Services in Preschools

The model programs that form the basis of our research evidence that preschools are cost-effective investments also provided comprehensive services. Especially for families in poverty, inattention to their social service needs may obfuscate the efforts of the educational curriculum. Unfortunately, it is precisely these services that were hardest hit during the Reagan administration.

Focusing on Preschool While Ignoring Other Ages

Experts such as Bernice Weissbourd (1987) from the Family Resource Coalition and Edward Zigler (1986) from Yale University note that societal intervention into the lives of at-risk children must begin with a concern for the mental and physical health of the pregnant woman and with the psychological well-being of the family into which the child is born. A growing number of studies are beginning to document the positive effects of family-support programs, and several states are beginning to create these programs (Powell, 1986; Meyerhoff & White, 1986). It is laudable that the Committee for Economic Development recommends programs to encourage teen parents to remain in school, and health care for high-risk mothers and children, as well as parenting education programs.

In addition, it is clear that quality child care programs are not only necessary in the preschool years. The Census report (U.S. Department of Commerce, Bureau of the Census, 1987) has documented the startling fact that 51% of the mothers of infants are in the labor force. Furthermore, the number of children left home to care for themselves alone or their younger siblings is unknown, but estimates put the number at more than two million. If one takes the perspective of the employed parent, the need for child care extends from infancy through early adolescence and is especially pronounced in the earliest years. While money for early childhood efforts is often in short supply, and states as well as the federal government may have to make choices about where to begin, it is important to realize that programs directed solely at preschool children may already be too late.

An Emphasis on Work/Family Initiatives

In addition to the development of early childhood programs, the pressure to have a maximally competitive work force has also resulted in the development of numerous work/family corporate initiatives by progressive employers. It is reasoned that the demographics of the current labor force have changed dramatically and will continue to do so. A large percentage of the present work force is caring for children and for elderly parents. Furthermore, the work force will be increasingly female. The Hudson Institute, in a report entitled *Work force 2000* prepared for the Department of Labor, estimates that 64% of all new entrants will be female, stating that "only 15% of the new entrants to the labor force over the next 13 years will be native white males, compared to 47% in that category today" (Johnston, 1987, p. 1). Seventy percent of the women currently in the work force are in the child-bearing years, and 80% of these employees are expected to have children during their work life (Galinsky & Friedman, 1986). In addition, the work force will also be increasingly minority and aging (Johnston, 1987).

In response to such demographic realities, The Hudson Institute (Johnston, 1987) recommends six policy challenges. One of these is to help workers balance the demands of work and family life.

> What is needed is a thoroughgoing reform of the institutions and policies that govern the workplace, to insure that women can participate fully in the economy, and that men and women have the time and resources needed to invest in their children. (p. 13)

The Range of Work/Family Initiatives

In the 1980s, a growing number of companies began a process of reform in which the programs and policies developed fell within five business functions:

1. *Time Policies*: Corporations have developed more flexible work arrangements, such as flexitime and flexiplace.
2. *Leave Policies*: Businesses are providing paid and unpaid leaves for childbirth, parenting, the care of young children, or other personal or family matters. They include maternity leaves, parenting and adoptive parenting leaves, time banks, personal leaves, and personal days off.
3. *Benefits*: Businesses are revamping their benefits away from a model that assumes the work force consists of traditional families in which one parent is at home to provide caregiving, to a model that recognizes the diversity of today's families. Such policies include Cafeteria Benefit Plans, Flexible Savings Accounts (salaries are reduced to pay for child care or other family needs with pretax dollars), or Long-Term Care Insurance to pay for the long-term health care of oneself, elderly parents, or a spouse.
4. *Dependent Care Policies*: Companies are establishing programs to help employees provide for the care of their children or their elderly parents. These include resource and referral programs to help employees find child care or elder care services, on- or near-site child care programs, or employee discounts or vouchers to help pay the cost of elder or child care.
5. *Other Educational or Wellness Services*: Companies are providing Employee Assistance Programs, wellness programs, and relocation counseling that may be used by other family members. They also sponsor educational seminars at the workplace on balancing work and family life, peer

support groups, and training for supervisors to make them more attuned to the work/family problems of employees.

The growth in the number of companies providing family-friendly programs has been high. According to the Conference Board, 3,500 out of 6 million companies assisted employees with their child care needs in 1988 as compared to 110 companies in 1978 (Friedman, 1988). A recent survey of more than 1,500 human resource professionals conducted in the spring of 1988 by the American Society of Personnel Administration (ASPA) has a higher estimate: 10% of companies nationwide provide direct support for child care. They also assert that almost half of the companies in the U.S. are considering developing child care assistance programs. The prevalence of other family-friendly policies varies widely. ASPA found that 27% offer family stress counseling, with 10% considering it. Sixty-eight percent offer paid disability/maternity leave. In contrast to this figure, a recent nationwide study in nearly 100 communities conducted by the National Council of Jewish Women (1987) found that in 31% of the groups surveyed women receive less than 8 weeks of job-protected medical leave for maternity, and in over half of these groups women receive no job-protected leave at all. ASPA (1988) also finds that flexitime and part-time work are common work/family initiatives. They estimate that more than one third of all American companies offer flexitime.

The Types of Companies that Develop Work/Family Programs

The predictors of which companies are likely to develop work/family programs or policies have not yet been firmly established. However, our research team is currently conducting a study to identify these factors. Dana Friedman (1983) and others have found that such companies are likely to be headed by younger, entrepreneurial management, to be in a business (such as health care) that is not inconsistent with the provision of work/family programs, to be nonunionized, and to be in a community where other employers are also developing work/family programs. Friedman found, as did the ASPA, that such companies are the larger employers nationwide.

It is generally assumed that a lack of personal experience with work/family programs on the part of senior management inhibits the development of work/family initiatives (Burden & Googins, 1986). The

film *Walking the Tightrope* produced by the Bureau of National Affairs
for a 1987 Department of Labor Conference ends with the statement
that this country will see a surge in the development of work/family
initiatives "when the CEO is pregnant." Bank Street research at Merck
& Co., Inc. indicates that personal experience is not necessarily linked
to support for the development of programs on the part of decision
makers. More predictive is leadership style (Galinsky, 1986). The least
interested managers were absorbed in their own tasks and less inclined
to care about their subordinates beyond their job performance. The
managers most likely to champion this cause were similar to the managers described by Peters and Waterman (1982) in *In Search of Excellence* as those who "walk around." They knew their employees as
people, saw them as capable of future growth, and felt that they would
perform more productively if they were treated with respect.

Work/Family Initiatives and Productivity

When we have asked employers informally why they develop work/
family initiatives, they are likely to say "for bottom line reasons." They
assert that today's work force is having greater conflict in balancing
work and family responsibilities and that programs can potentially
reduce this conflict, helping employees be more productive on the job.
Greater productivity is especially needed in such competitive times.

Do family-responsive policies increase employees' productivity?
There have been three studies that have looked at employers' perception
of the benefits of corporate child care programs. In a study conducted
by Perry (1982) of 59 employers (predominantly hospitals with on-site
centers), 88% of the employers indicated that the program increased
their ability to attract employees, 72% noted lower absenteeism, and
65% felt that it improved the employees' attitude toward the employer.
In a study by Magid (1983) of 204 companies with child care programs,
employers ranked the top benefits as improved ability to recruit, improved morale, and lowered absenteeism. A survey of 178 companies
(Burud, Aschbacher, & McCroskey, 1984), found that 90% of the
managers thought their company's program had improved morale, 85%
felt that the company's ability to recruit had been affected positively,
and 85% felt public relations had been more positive.

A 1987 study by the National Council of Jewish Women is one of the
first that shows direct links between a family-friendly work environment and benefits for employers. This study evaluated the extent to

which employers accommodated the needs and concerns of pregnant workers. Eight indicators of accommodation were measured: sick leave, disability leave for maternity, wage replacement during disability leave, parental leave, health insurance coverage, flexible scheduling, supportiveness of supervisors, and child care assistance. When employers were more accommodating, pregnant workers were more satisfied with their jobs, took fewer sick days, worked more on their own time, worked later into pregnancy, and were more likely to return to their jobs after childbirth.

To date, we have much more to learn about the relationship between work/family policies and productivity. Currently, the Bank Street research team is conducting a study with a human resource cost-accounting aspect that can measure precisely the cost-benefit ratio of work/family programs. When companies begin to conduct systematic evaluations of their own work/family programs, our knowledge base will certainly broaden.

A Potential Pitfall: Ignoring Work Conditions

Before widespread evaluations of the programs are made, however, it is imperative to go back to the substantial data base that has been accumulated on the nature of work/family problems in order to assess whether the solutions address the problems.

For the most part, the answer to this inquiry is affirmative. For example, one of the recurrent sources of work/family stress in the literature is related to time pressures. Researchers have found that a lack of time flexibility is indeed associated with negative psychological outcomes (Piotrkowski & Katz, 1983; Bohen & Viveros-Long, 1981; Staines & Pleck, 1983). Additionally, we have found in our various studies that employees who work longer hours are more likely to feel more conflict between work/family responsibilities, have higher levels of stress, and experience more stress-related health problems (Galinsky & Hughes, 1987; Hughes & Galinsky, 1988). The numerous corporate programs that have been aimed at providing more time flexibility, therefore, do address a major source of stress.

Another positive example is child care. Research strongly indicates that problems in locating, obtaining, maintaining, and paying for child care affect parents on the job (Galinsky, 1988a). Thus presumably, the numerous corporate initiatives relating to child care that have been developed do ease these conflicts.

It is important to note, however, that virtually no work/family initiatives have been aimed at changing the nature of the jobs, although certain job conditions (such as having a demanding and hectic job) are among the strongest predictors of the worker's physical and mental well-being. For example, Karasek (1979) found that demanding jobs are associated with poorer health. Our research has replicated his results. We have found that when workers feel rushed and have more to do than they feel they can accomplish, they are more likely to report more stress, more stress-related health problems, and experience greater conflict between job and family responsibilities (Galinsky, Hughes, & Shinn, 1986; Hughes & Galinsky, 1987; Galinsky, Love, Bragonier, & Hughes, 1987).

Another job condition that emerges as significant is a lack of job autonomy. When workers feel that they have little control over resolving the job problems they face, they are less likely to be satisfied at work and at home and have a lower sense of well-being (Piotrkowski & Crits-Christoph, 1982). Karasek's work reveals that when employees have a hectic job with little autonomy, they are at a greater risk for job dissatisfaction, stress, and even heart disease (Karasek, 1979; Karasek, Baker, Marxer, Ahlbom, & Theorell, 1981). Our research at Bank Street has revealed that tension from these job conditions can spill over into the employee's family life, resulting in more irritability, less energy, and more negative moods which can affect the employee's satisfaction with marital and parenting relationships (Hughes & Galinsky, 1987).

While improving undesirable work conditions has been a part of work reform movements such as Quality of Worklife and Quality Circles, it has never been as integral to the work/family field. Yet data reveals that such issues are far from peripheral but are, in fact, central. There is one issue, however, that companies are beginning to include as a work/family issue: the relationship between the supervisor and supervisee. Research fully supports this notion. For example, House (1981) found that the relationship with the supervisor mediates between job conditions and employee's health and well-being. Repetti (1985), likewise, found the lack of supervisor support was linked to anxiety and depression.

The research to date, however, has focused on the supervisor's support in terms of work roles; that is, the ability to communicate, to monitor, to provide clear expectations and feedback, and so forth. The studies that we have been conducting at Bank Street indicate that another aspect of the supervisor's role is linked to employee well-being: the supervisor's support when work/family problems arise. Over the course of numerous studies, we have developed a measure of supervisor work/family support that assesses the degree to which the supervisor knows the company's work/family policies, is fair in implementation, and is flexible when work/family problems occur. Our studies reveal that having a supervisor who provides work/family support is associated with lower levels of stress and fewer stress-related health problems (Galinsky, 1988b). Thus having family-friendly policies is one matter, but how these policies are interpreted and implemented, and thus their effectiveness, depends upon the immediate supervisor.

In many workplaces, however, the supervisor may not have much power. He or she may want to give a parent permission to stay at home with an acutely ill child, for example, but is prevented from doing so because of company policy. On the basis of numerous focus groups, we developed a measure of the corporate work/family culture, assessing the degree to which job security and advancement are perceived as antithetical to expressing a commitment to one's work/family needs. In recent assessments in two corporations, we have found that experiencing a nonsupportive work/family culture is linked to poor outcomes in mental and physical well-being. In fact, this variable seems to be one of our most powerful predictors of work/family conflict and stress (Galinsky, 1988b).

The Emergence of a New Phase in Work/Family Initiatives

Business efforts to address the issue of supervisor work/family support and the corporate work/family culture are few and far between. However, a survey we are in the process of conducting of 284 companies and their human resource policies has revealed that the most innovative companies have turned to these issues, ushering in what is termed Phase II in corporate responsiveness to work/family issues. In Phase I, companies identified a problem (e.g., employees having trouble finding and paying for child care) and then developed a policy or program to resolve it (in this case, setting up a resource and referral program or providing child care discounts). In Phase I, there were a few hundred pioneering companies that blazed the trail.

In Phase II, those same pioneering companies have taken the next step. They are dealing with more difficult, less tangible issues such as the need to provide greater time flexibility, to train supervisors to be more supportive to the work/family concerns of today's work force, and to change the corporate culture to be more family-friendly. In addition, in these exemplary companies, top management is addressing work/ family issues as a legitimate rather than a peripheral business concern. Finally, business functions which used to be seen as separate (benefits, training, personal leave policies) are being re-evaluated together to assess the impact of various policies on one another and on employees' ability to manage their work and family responsibilities.

In Phase II, more and more companies are becoming involved—not just the pioneers, but those who state, "We don't want to be first." A final characteristic of Phase II is that there is more emphasis on companies collaborating in joint problem-solving and program development. For example, a group of employers in Linn-Benton Counties in Oregon conducted a community needs assessment and are in the process of creating a community child care resource and referral service. And, in New York City, a group of employers have joined together to develop a facility to provide short-term emergency care.

An Irony

In the development of work/family initiatives, the need of the company for a more productive work force and the need of individual employees for a better quality of family life with less work/family stress are in synch. Families can benefit, as can companies, from providing greater time flexibility and dependent care assistance. However, there are limits to this harmony. A company in a competitive mode needs workers to push, to work longer hours, to travel, and to speed up production lines. Companies may want employees to be present on the job when those employees may want to be home with a sick child or an elderly parent. These are the issues that will engage us in the coming years.

In addition, a productivity effort can lead some companies to adopt work/family initiatives while others, under the same pressures, cut back on employee benefits, downsize, and become "lean and mean." How these different paths will affect business and families in the short and long terms requires further investigation.

Conclusion

In conclusion, the competitive policies of the business community have spotlighted problems in today's and tomorrow's labor forces, stimulating business interest in the early education of young children and in the development of work/family efforts. If the complexity of these issues is not addressed, however, the intended goals may not be achieved. If early education programs neglect the child care needs of employed parents or provide inappropriate learning experiences, then the future labor force may not be up to the challenges that lie ahead. If work/family efforts ignore the nature of the job itself or the way such programs are implemented by supervisors, the effects of such programs may be diminished. We are at a crossroad. The impact of today's competitive policies may provide children with firmer early childhood backgrounds and diminish the work/family stress of their parents, or the opposite may occur. This is our challenge.

References

American Society for Personnel Administration. (1988). *Employers and child care: The human resource professional's view*. [Executive Summary]. Alexandria, VA: Author.

Berruta-Clement, J. R., Schweinhart, L. J., Barnett, W. S., Epstein, A. S., & Weikart, D. P. (1984). Changed lives: The effects of the Perry Preschool Program on youths through age 19. *Monographs of the High/Scope Educational Research Foundation, 8*.

Bohen, H. H., & Viveros-Long, A. (1981). *Balancing jobs and family life: Do flexible work schedules help?* Philadelphia, PA: Temple University Press.

Burden, D., & Googins, B. (1986). *Boston University balancing job and homelife study*. Boston, MA: Boston University School of Social Work.

Burud, S., Aschbacher, P., & McCroskey, J. (1984). *Employer-supported child care: Investing in human resources*. Boston, MA: Auburn House.

Committee for Economic Development, Research and Policy Committee. (1987). *Children in need: Investment strategies for the educationally disadvantaged*. [Executive summary]. New York, NY: Author.

Commissioner's Task Force on the Education of Children and Youth At Risk. (1988, September). *The time for assertive action: School strategies for promoting the educational success of at-risk children*. [Draft report.] Albany: The State Education Department, The University of the State of New York.

Cummings, E. M. (1986, April). *Caregiver stability in day care: Continuity vs. daily association*. Paper presented at the International Conference on Infant Studies, Los Angeles, CA.

Friedman, D. E. (1983). *Encouraging employer support to working parents.* New York: Carnegie Corporation of New York.

Friedman, D. E. (1988). Estimates from the Conference Board and other national monitors of employer-supported child care. [Unpublished memo.] New York, NY: The Conference Board.

Galinsky, E. (1986). Family life and corporate policies. In M. Yogman & T. B. Brazelton (Eds.), *In support of families.* Cambridge, MA: Harvard University Press.

Galinsky, E. (1988a, March). *Child care and productivity.* Paper prepared for the Child Care Action Campaign conference, Child Care: The Bottom Line, New York, NY.

Galinsky, E. (1988b, August). *The impact of supervisors' attitudes and company culture on work/family adjustment.* Paper presented at the Annual Convention of the American Psychological Association, Atlanta, GA.

Galinsky, E., & Friedman, D. E. (1986). *Investing in quality child care: A report for AT&T.* Basking Ridge, NJ: AT&T.

Galinsky, E., & Hughes, D. (1987, August). *The Fortune Magazine child care study.* Paper presented at the Annual Convention of the American Psychological Association, New York, NY.

Galinsky, E., Hughes, D., & Shinn, M. (1986). *The corporate work and family life study.* [In-depth study.] Unpublished paper, Bank Street College of Education, New York, NY.

Galinsky, E., Love, M., Bragonier, P. H., & Hughes, D. (1987). *The family study.* Foundation report, Bank Street College of Education, New York, NY.

Hofferth, S. L., & Phillips, D. A. (1987). Child care in the United States, 1970-1995. *Journal of Marriage and the Family, 49*, 559-571.

House, J. S. (1981). *Work stress and social support.* Reading, MA: Addison-Wesley.

Howes, C. (1988, April). *Can the age of entry and the quality of infant child care predict behaviors in kindergarten?* Paper presented at the International Conference on Infant Studies, Washington, DC.

Hughes, D. (1987, August). *Child care and working parents.* Paper presented at the Annual Convention of the American Psychological Association, New York, NY.

Hughes, D., & Galinsky, E. (1987). *Relationships between job characteristics, work/family interference, and marital adjustment.* Unpublished manuscript.

Hughes, D., & Galinsky, E. (1988). Balancing work and family life: Research and corporate application. In A. E. Gottfried & A. W. Gottfried (Eds.). *Maternal employment and children's development: Longitudinal research.* New York, NY: Plenum Press.

Human capital, (1988, September 19). *Business Week*, cover.

Johnston, W. B. (1987). *Work force 2000: Work and workers for the 21st century.* [Executive Summary]. Indianapolis, IN: Hudson Institute.

Karasek, R. A. (1979). Job demands, job decision latitude, and mental strain: Implications for job redesign. *Administrative Science Quarterly, 24*, 285-308.

Karasek, R. A., Baker, R., Marxer, F., Ahlbom, A., & Theorell, T. (1981). Job decision latitude, job demands, and cardiovascular disease: A prospective study of Swedish men. *American Journal of Public Health, 71*, 694-705.

Kozol, J. (1985). *Illiterate America*. Garden City, NY: Anchor Press/Doubleday.

Lally, J. R., Mangione, P. L., & Honig, A. S. (1987). *Long range impact of early intervention on low-income children and their families*. Syracuse, NY: The Syracuse University Family Research Program.

Lurie, R., Galinsky, E., & Hughes, D. (1988). [Resources for Child Care Management (RCCM)—Bank Street College of Education needs assessments.] Unpublished raw data.

Magid, R. Y. (1983). *Child care initiatives for working parents: Why employers get involved*. New York, NY: American Management Association.

Mitchell, A. (1988). *The public school early childhood study: The district survey*. Bank Street College of Education, New York, NY.

Meyerhoff, M. K., & White, B. L. (1986, September). Making the grade as parents. *Psychology Today*, pp. 38-45.

National Council of Jewish Women (1987, November). *Accommodating pregnancy in the workplace*. NCJW Center for the Child Report, November, 1987. New York, NY: National Council of Jewish Women.

Perry, K. (1982). *Employers and child care: Establishing services through the workplace*. Washington, DC: Women's Bureau, U.S. Department of Labor.

Peters, T. J., & Waterman, R. H., Jr. (1983). *In search of excellence*. New York, NY: Warner Books.

Piotrkowski, C. S., & Crits-Christoph, P. (1982). Women's jobs and family adjustment. In J. Aldous (Ed.), *Two paychecks: Life in dual-earner families*. Beverly Hills, CA: Sage Publications.

Piotrkowski, C. S., & Katz, M. H. (1983). Work experience and family relations among working class and lower middle-class families. In H. Z. Lopata & J. H. Pleck (Eds.), *Research in the interweave of social roles: Families and jobs* (vol. 3). Greenwich, CT: JAI Press.

Powell, D. (1986). Parent education and support programs. *Young Children, 41*(3), 47-53.

Repetti, R. L. (1985). *Social factors in the workplace and mental health*. Paper presented at the Annual Convention of the American Psychological Association, Los Angeles, CA.

Select Committee on Children, Youth, and Families. (1984). *Families and child care: Improving the options*. Washington, DC: U.S. Government Printing Office.

Shinn, M., Ortiz-Torres, B., Morris, A., Simko, P., & Wong, N. (1987, August). *Child care patterns, stress, and job behaviors among working parents*. Paper presented at the Annual Convention of the American Psychological Association, New York, NY.

Smith, R. E. (Ed.). (1979). *The subtle revolution*. Washington, DC: The Urban Institute.

Staines, G. L., & Pleck, J. H. (1983). *The impact of work schedules on the family*. Ann Arbor: The University of Michigan Institute of Social Research.

U.S. Department of Commerce, Bureau of the Census (1987). *Estimates of the population of the United States by age, sex, and race: 1980-1986*. Current population reports series, P-25, no. 1000. Washington, DC: U.S. Government Printing Office.

U.S. Department of Education. (1988). *Report of the Office of Planning, Budget, & Evaluation*. Washington, DC: Author.

U.S. Department of Labor (1988, April). *Child care: A work force issue.* (Secretary's Task Force on Child Care.) Washington, DC: U.S. Department of Labor.

Whitebook, M., Pemberton, C., Lombardi, J., Galinsky, E., Bellm, D., & Fillinger, B. (1988). *Raising salaries: Strategies that work.* Berkeley, CA: Child Care Employee Project.

Weissbourd, B. (1987). A brief history of family support. In S. L. Kagan, D. R. Powell, B. Weissbourd, & E. Zigler (Eds.), *America's family support programs* (pp. 38-56). New Haven, CT: Yale University Press.

Zigler, E. (1986, September). *The future of the family resource movement.* Speech given at The Family Resource Coalition's national conference, *Family Resource Movement: Changing Families, Changing Responses*, Chicago, IL.

9 A Case Study in Effective Organization Change Toward High Involvement Management

LEONARD D. GOODSTEIN

The world in which American business and industry finds itself has changed radically in the past two decades. These changes in both the internal and external organizational environments in which organizations must operate require continual changes in the organizations for vitality and even survival.

Organizational change, however, is difficult to plan and execute. The management of such change is facilitated by an understanding of organizations as open social systems and the use of such understanding in the design and management of the change process. Yet most managers lack such a conceptual grasp of their organizations and fail either to understand or use such an open systems approach in their management of change. The present analysis is offered as an overview of a psychological approach to organizational change and how psychology and psychologists can play a role in the facilitation of the change process.

Beginning with an analysis of organizations as open social systems— an approach that I have found both provocative and useful in my own work—I then will discuss organizational change and review psychologically based change processes, using throughout a case study of a successful organization change that illustrates many of these issues.

Adapted, in part, from the author's (1988) "Social psychology of the workplace." In I. Cohen (Ed.), The G. Stanley Hall Lecture Series (Vol. 8). Washington, DC: American Psychological Association.

The assistance of Jeanette Treat Goodstein and W. Warner Burke in the preparation of this chapter is gratefully acknowledged.

Organizations as Open Social Systems

The term "organization" is not easy to define. It is so difficult, in fact, that March and Simon (1958), two leading students of organizations, declined to offer a definition in their classic book. Instead, they noted, "it is easier, and probably more useful, to give examples of formal organizations than to define the term" (p. 1). Undeterred by such advice, I believe that a useful working definition is possible: *An organization is a group (or groups) of individuals who regularly interact together to achieve some shared explicit purpose or goal through the expenditure of differentiated and coordinated effort.*

My formal definition of an organization emphasizes that an organization may involve single or multiple groups. There must also be some regular pattern of activity, a clear goal towards which all are striving, and both a division of labor and some integration of that divided effort. If any of these conditions are lacking, the organization is unlikely to achieve its goals. This definition thus encompasses all business, educational, religious, social, and political organizations regardless of their size and complexity. (I leave it to the reader to decide whether or not this definition is sufficiently inclusive to comprehend the typical American family.) What is most evident about this definition, at least from my point of view, is that it clearly describes the organization as a social system.

All social systems, including organizations, involve the behavior of individuals in regular patterns of activity. This pattern of behaviors needs to be relatively constant, regularly repeated, and interdependent if organizational goals are to be achieved. If the pattern of behavior occurs only rarely or unpredictably, there is no organization. This is *not* to say that the goals of the individuals are the same as those of their organization, but rather that the achievement of the individual goals must facilitate the achievement of organizational goals and purposes.

Open Systems Theory

Open system theory (Katz & Kahn, 1978; Katz, 1986) provides an especially valuable approach to understanding organizations as social systems. Open systems theory suggests that social systems are best understood as patterns of recurrent activities in which energy (information, raw materials, human resources, and so on) is imported into the system and transformed with the resulting product then exported back into the environment. Open systems theory focuses upon the structure of systems and on the relationships between the structural elements of the systems, especially on the interdependence of these elements as each affects the energy transformation process.

Open systems theory has been advanced as a clear alternative to closed systems approaches, that is, systems that operate according to classical Newtonian principles. In contrast to closed systems, open systems maintain themselves through continual exchanges of energy between the internal and external environments. This continual interaction with the environment means that the system or organization cannot internally determine its desired outcomes. Rather, the external environment will play a major role in such determinations and will incidentally produce a good bit of situational uncertainty.

Bureaucracies are the classic example of organizations as closed systems—a term coined by Weber (1924/1947) as a label for organizations characterized by impersonality and rationality—where rules cover all contingencies; where technically expert supervisors act as impartial autocrats; and where communications follow a carefully controlled, hierarchical path. Bureaucratic and other closed systems models of organizations tend to emphasize heavily their formal structure, while organizations using the open systems model approach heavily emphasize their informal structure.

Peters (1988) has provided a useful visual representation of a closed systems organization which he characterized as an "inflexible, rule-determined mass producer of the past" (p. 106). The corporate center is responsible for policy, communications are one-way, and supposedly impermeable boundaries separate organizational units from each other and from the corporate center. It is an orderly system, one in which all persons know their places. This is in sharp contrast to Peters' representation of an open system organization, which he characterized as "flexible, porous, adaptive, . . . and constantly improving everything." The open system is guided by its vision and values rather than by rules; communications are open; and boundaries are readily permeable, both internally and externally. While Peters' representation of an open system is messy, almost chaotic, it is a far better representation of how successful organizations actually do operate in today's competitive world.

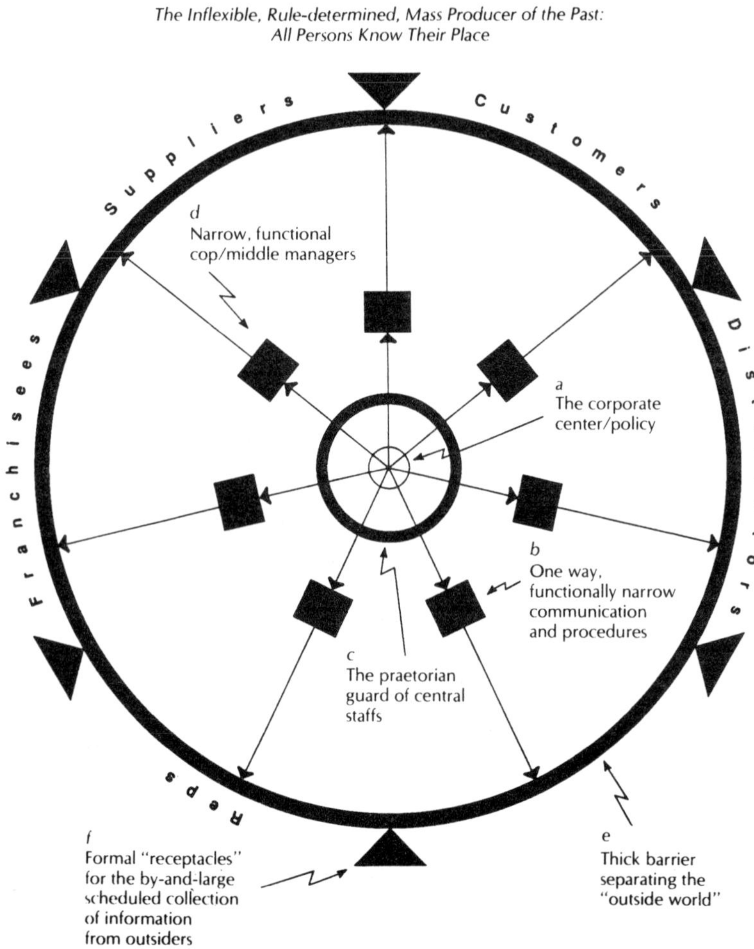

The Inflexible, Rule-determined, Mass Producer of the Past:
All Persons Know Their Place

Figure 9.1. A Graphic Representation of "the inflexible, rule-determined mass producer of the past."

SOURCE: Peters, T. (1988). Restoring American competitiveness: Looking for new models of organization. (p. 311).

The functioning of any open system consists of recurring cycles of input, transformation, and output. Although this transformation process is an internal one, both the input and output involve active dealings with the external environment. To function effectively, a system must mon-

The Flexible, Porous, Adaptive, Fleet-of-Foot Organization of the Future:
Every Person is "Paid" to be Obstreperous, a Disrespecter of Formal Boundaries,
to Hustle and to Be Engaged Fully with Engendering Swift Action, Constantly Improving Everything

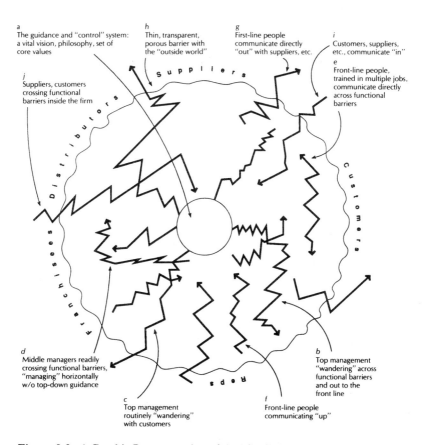

a
The guidance and "control" system:
a vital vision, philosophy, set of
core values

h
Thin, transparent,
porous barrier with
the "outside world"

g
First-line people
communicate directly
"out" with suppliers, etc.

i
Customers, suppliers,
etc., communicate "in"

e
Front-line people,
trained in multiple jobs,
communicate directly
across functional
barriers

j
Suppliers, customers
crossing functional
barriers inside the firm

d
Middle managers readily
crossing functional barriers,
"managing" horizontally
w/o top-down guidance

b
Top management
"wandering" across
functional barriers
and out to the
front line

c
Top management
routinely "wandering"
with customers

f
Front-line people
communicating "up"

Figure 9.2. A Graphic Representation of the "flexible, porous, adaptive
organization of the future."

SOURCE: Peters, T. (1988). Restoring American competitiveness: Looking for new models of
organizations. (p. 313).

itor the external environment to assure that it can adequately manage
the input from the environment and that the environment can manage
the output from the system. A competent organization clearly is one that
engages in such environmental surveillance on a regular basis.

As an example of this recurring cycle, a manufacturing organization must be able to regularly secure the necessary raw materials, power, machinery, and workers in order to transform these resources into product lines that the environment is willing to accept and able to purchase when available. Similarly, a university has its own annual cycle: it admits new students at the beginning of each academic year, transforms them into educated persons over a period of several years, and graduates them into an accepting society. In both examples, we can observe the cyclic nature of these processes, the need for a match between the input and output characteristics, and the constant exchange with the environment.

An open system can be effective only when it restricts its input to what it can handle and similarly restricts its output to what the environment can accept. Thus the manufacturer must avoid overbuying raw material, overexpanding plant capacity, and overhiring too many workers on the one hand; and producing more products than there are willing customers on the other. Similarly, the university must be certain that it has enough teachers and dorm rooms for its student body and that it requires a sufficient level of academic performance of its graduates to give them marketplace credibility. Again, the competent organization has in place the necessary mechanisms to ensure that this organization/environment match occurs.

This open system approach highlights two aspects of organizations as social systems: (1) action in one part of the system predictably leads to action in other parts of the system, and (2) organizations typically are in a state of constant flux as a result of their openness to environmental inputs. The open system approach treats organizations like complex living organisms rather than static mechanistic systems.

Organizational Structure

Human organizations lack structure in any anatomical sense; rather, they are held together by patterns of behavioral events that give them stability and order. The most important of these patterns are the *role* behaviors of the organization's members, the organization's *norms* prescribing and sanctioning these behaviors, and the *values* in which roles and norms are embedded. Roles are sets of functionally specific, interrelated behaviors generated by interconnected tasks. Such role behaviors are carried out not because of the individual's personal needs but because these behaviors are necessary for system functioning.

In all organizations these roles become quickly accepted and habitual for those who occupy them. Thus, from an open systems perspective, organizations can be seen as a series of interrelated and overlapping roles. Each of these roles is interdependent with the others, allowing the organization to maintain its viability—that is, teachers cannot survive without students, supervisors without supervisees, and so on. From such a perspective, organizations are structures of roles.

In a similar vein, Moch (1980) argued that the only real structure of an organization is to be found in the network of integrated relationships among that organization's workers. Meyer and Rowan (1977) went even further in their theoretical analysis, insisting that the institutional or formal realities of an organization's structure exist more in its myths and ceremonies than in its formal organizational design. Ransom, Hinings, and Greenwood (1980) stated that the *process* of structuring is a more relevant issue than is the more static and mechanistic concept of structure. All of these writers emphasize the fact that organizations need to be understood in a more dynamic sense than is typically provided by the traditional organization chart.

Once we accept the importance of roles in organizations, we can readily understand why these roles are embedded in strong belief systems about how these roles should be carried out. Powerful sanctions maintain what is seen as appropriate role behavior or *norms*. Statements such as, "That's the way we do it around here," "Our way or the highway," and "That's simply not the XYZ way of doing business," are simply among the most obvious examples of the sanctions brought to bear on organizational deviants. Thus norms and values are those commonly held beliefs of an evaluative nature that support and maintain role behavior. *Values* tend to be the more generalized belief systems, and norms the more behaviorally specific.

The Informal Organization

These values, norms, and roles coupled with the unstructured pattern of friendships, groupings, and communication networks found in all organizations constitute the *informal organization*. In contrast, the *formal organization* is the official blueprint of how work is to be done; but it is never fully realized in the behavior of the organization's members. The formal organization typically tends to ignore the informal organization, whereas the informal structure often serves to protect organizational members from the formal structure or at least to reduce its potency in governing the day-to-day behavior of its members.

The seminal research project of Roethlisberger and Dickson (1939)—the so-called Hawthorne studies—played a central role in initially identifying the critical importance of the informal organization. This research was intended to assess the impact of a variety of working conditions such as rest periods, pay incentives, and lighting on worker productivity, but its overwhelming significance was in its demonstration that such factors were clearly less important than various psychological factors that emerged. The most important of these was the strong sense of group cohesion and identity exhibited by those who were included in each of the several experimental conditions. These groups quickly formed norms about how they would respond to the experimental interventions, norms that affected the behavior and roles of individual workers and thus the outcome of the experiment.

The outcome of the Hawthorne studies is often misrepresented in psychology and other textbooks (Bramel & Friend, 1981) as demonstrating across-the-board increases in productivity regardless of the experimental conditions, primarily as a result of the attention paid to the workers by the experimenters. The true "Hawthorne effect," however, is that these workers—like all of us—developed a group dynamic, one that set the production norms in each of the conditions. This early finding on the importance of the effects of group norms on member behavior has been largely supported by innumerable laboratory and field studies conducted since.

Another seminal study (Coch & French, 1948) found that workers more readily accepted changes in work rules when they had either directly or indirectly participated in planning the changes, a finding also extensively replicated over the years. In the Coch and French study, participation facilitated the development of the new work processes as a group goal accepted and worked toward by the group. It is interesting to note that whereas participation through representation was effective in producing acceptance, direct participation produced greater and earlier performance changes. Direct participation probably produced better understanding of the nature of the changes and a higher sense of involvement.

Some Real-World Implications

Of greatest practical importance, however, are the changes in corporate America's attitudes toward the social psychology of the workplace. Buffeted at home and abroad by foreign competition that appears to produce higher quality goods at lower prices, corporate America has now largely forsaken (at least publicly and momentarily) its traditional analogy of the organization and its members as a machine and parts designed to work effectively and efficiently. Instead, many American corporations are accepting the "New Age" view of organizations as "a nested set of open, living systems and subsystems dependent upon the larger environment for survival" (Waldbaum, 1987, p. 19). What is surprising about this quote is not this view, which has been normative in the organizational psychology literature for several decades, but its source: *The Wall Street Journal.* And it is typical to find such articles in virtually every issue of most recent American business publications: articles on corporate culture, on the changing values and attitudes of American workers, on the need for greater employee participation in managerial decision making, and on the place of employees as an important (if not the most important) asset of the corporation.

No one—certainly not I—would ever suggest that there are no longer any traditionally managed organizations in America. However, corporate executives definitely have begun to recognize that managing the social psychology of the workplace is a critical element in the success of any organization. Kenneth H. Olsen, Chairman of Digital Equipment Corporation (a leading computer manufacturer of which he is the founder), clearly recognized this in his 1987 commencement address to the Massachusetts Institute of Technology. He suggests that some of the most satisfying activities in running a business are "to help others to be creative, to take responsibility, to be challenged in their jobs, and to be successful" (Olsen, 1987).

This view of organizations as social systems has important implications for both the theory and practice of organizational change. As we have seen, the human element is an important consideration in any change effort if that effort is to be successful.

Organizational Change: The Case of British Airways

Organizations are in a constant state of change, much to the chagrin of both those who prefer stability to change and those who elect to use a closed systems model for understanding organizational life. On the other hand, such continual change does satisfy those who follow an open systems approach to understanding organizations and who prefer a bit more excitement in day-to-day organizational life.

Organizations tend to change primarily because of external pressures rather than because of some internal desire or need to change. A few all-too-familiar examples of the kinds of environmental factors requiring organizations to change are when a new competitor snares a significant portion of a firm's market share, an old customer is acquired by a giant conglomerate that dictates new sales arrangements, or a new invention offers the possibility of changing the existing production technology of the organization. Other examples include new government regulations that affect certain health-care financing programs, or economic and social conditions that create long-term changes in the availability of the labor force. Each of these external changes requires the competent organization to be alert to early warning signs and to move promptly to make the necessary internal changes required to remain viable in the changing external world.

For the past five years, I have been involved as a consultant in a large-scale change effort at British Airways (BA). In 1982, the Thatcher government made a decision to convert BA from government to private ownership. BA had regularly required large subsidies from the government (almost $900 million in 1982); subsidies that the government felt it should not provide. Even more importantly, the Conservative government was ideologically opposed to government ownership of businesses they regarded as the appropriate province of private enterprise. The growing deregulation of international air traffic was another important environmental change. Air fares were no longer fixed, and the resulting price wars placed BA at even greater risk of financial losses.

In order to be able to "privatize," that is, sell BA shares on the London stock exchange, it was necessary to make BA profitable. The pressures thus exerted on BA by the external environment were broad and intense. It was these external pressures that led to the massive change effort in which I and dozens of other consultants have been involved.

The internal organizational changes, driven by these external pressures, have been massive and widespread. They have transformed the

THE BA SUCCESS STORY
Creating the "World's Favourite Airline"

	1982	1987
OWNERSHIP	Government	Private
PROFIT/(LOSS)	($900 million)	$435 million
CULTURE	Bureaucratic and militaristic	Service-oriented and market-driven
PASSENGER LOAD FACTOR	Decreasing	Increasing—up 16% 1st quarter 1988
CARGO LOAD	Stable	Increasing—up 41% 1st quarter 1988
SHARE PRICE	N/A	Increased 67% (2/11/87–8/11/87)
ACQUISITIONS	N/A	British Caledonian

Figure 9.3. A Contrast of the British Airways Performance from 1982 to 1988.

BA culture from what BA managers described as bureaucratic and militaristic to one that is now described as service oriented and market driven. The success of these efforts is clearly reflected in the data presented in Figure 9.3.

Figure 9.3 reflects the new mission of BA in its new advertising slogan—"The World's Favourite Airline." In the five years since the change effort was initiated, BA successfully did move from government to private ownership, and both passenger and cargo revenues have dramatically increased, leading to a substantial increase in share price over the offering price despite the market crash of October 1987. And, late in 1987, BA acquired British Caledonian Airways, its chief domestic competitor. The steps through which this transformation was accomplished clearly fit Lewin's (1958) model of the change process.

Lewin's Model of Change

According to the open systems view of organizations, they tend, like living creatures, to be homeostatic; that is, continuously working to maintain a steady state. This helps us to understand why organizations require external impetus for initiating change and, indeed, that change will be resisted even when it is necessary. There are three different levels at which organizational change can occur, each with different patterns of resistance to change; patterns that require different change strategies and techniques.

These levels are: (1) changing the *individuals* who work in the organization—that is their skills, values, attitudes, and eventually their behavior, but with such individual behavior change always regarded as instrumental to organizational change; (2) changing various organizational *structures and systems*—reward systems, reporting relationships, work design, and so on; and (3) directly changing the organizational *climate* or interpersonal style—how open people are with each other, how conflict is managed, how decisions are made, and so on (Porter, Lawler, & Hackman, 1975).

According to Lewin (1958), one of the pioneers in the field of the social psychology of organizations, the first step of any change process is *unfreezing* the present pattern of behavior as a way of managing resistance to change. Depending upon the organizational level of change intended, such unfreezing might involve selectively promoting or terminating employees on the individual level; developing highly experiential training programs about new organizational designs such as matrix management on the structural level; or providing data feedback about how employees feel about certain management practices on the climate level. Regardless of the level involved, however, each of these interventions is intended to make members of the organization address the organization's need for change, heighten their awareness about their own patterns of behavior, and make them more open to the change process.

The second step, *movement*, involves making the actual changes that will move the organization to another level of response. On the individual level, we would expect to see individuals behaving differently, perhaps demonstrating new skills or new supervisory practices. On the structural level, we would expect to see changes in actual organizational structures, reporting relationships, and reward systems that affect how people do their work. Finally, on the climate or interpersonal style level, we would expect to see patterns of behavior indicating greater interpersonal trust and openness and fewer dysfunctional interactions.

The final *refreezing* stage of the change process involves the stabilization or institutionalization of these changes—through the establishment of systems that make these behavioral patterns "relatively secure

APPLYING LEWIN'S MODEL TO THE BA CHANGE EFFORT

LEVELS	UNFREEZING	MOVEMENT	REFREEZING
INDIVIDUAL	New top management. Downsizing of top and middle management (59,000 to 37,000). "Putting People First."	Acceptance of concept of "emotional labor." Personnel staff as internal consultants. "Managing People First." Peer support groups.	Continued commitment of top management. Promotion of staff with new BA values. "Top Flight Academies." "Open Learning" programs.
STRUCTURES AND SYSTEMS	Use of diagonal task forces to plan change. Reduction in levels of hierarchy. Modification of budgeting process.	Profit sharing (3 weeks pay in 1987). Opening of Terminal 4. Purchase of Chartridge as training center. New "user friendly" MIS.	New performance appraisal system based upon both behavior and performance. Performance-based compensation system. Continued use of task forces.
CLIMATE/INTER-PERSONAL STYLE	Redefinition of the business: Service, not transportation. Top management commitment and involvement. Off-site team building meetings.	Trend toward decision-making at lowest possible level. Greater emphasis on open communications. Data feedback on management practices.	New livery and uniforms. New coat of arms. Development and use of cabin crew teams. Continued use of data feedback on management practices.

Figure 9.4. An Application of the Lewin (1958) Model to the British Airways Change Effort.

against change" (Lewin, 1958). This refreezing stage may involve redesigning the organization's recruitment process to assure that individuals who share the organization's new management style and value system are more likely to be selected. During the refreezing stage the organization may also ensure that the new behaviors have become the operating norms of work; that the reward system actually reinforces those behaviors; or that there is a new, more participative management style predominating.

According to Lewin, achieving lasting organizational change involves dealing with resistance to change through initially unblocking the present system. This unblocking usually involves some kind of confrontation (Beckhard, 1969) or retraining process. Then there must be planned behavior changes in the desired direction. Finally, deliberate steps need to be taken to cement these changes in place—the institutionalization of change—a process to make these changes semipermanent until the next cycle of change occurs.

Figure 9.4 presents an analysis of the BA change effort using Lewin's model. The many and diverse steps involved in the effort are categorized by stages—unfreezing, movement, and refreezing—and by level—individual, structures and systems, and climate/interpersonal style. While some might categorize one or more of the steps differently, I believe that the major steps are included and are correctly categorized.

The first step in unfreezing involved changing top management. In 1981, Lord King of Wartinbee, a senior British industrialist, was appointed Chairman of the Board and Colin Marshall, now Sir Colin, was appointed as CEO. The appointment of Marshall was itself a significant change in the BA culture. An outsider to BA, he came with a marketing background that was atypical of his predecessors, all of whom were retired senior Royal Air Force officers. It was Marshall who decided, shortly after his arrival, that the strategy of BA was to become "the World's Favourite Airline."

Shortly after the new strategy was announced, there was a massive reduction in the worldwide BA work force from 59,000 to 37,000. It is interesting to note that within a year after this staff reduction there was an improvement in virtually all BA performance indices: more on-time departures and arrivals, fewer out-of-service aircraft, less time on hold for telephone reservations, fewer lost bags, and so on. The consensus view at all levels within BA was that the downsizing had produced a reduction in the levels of the hierarchy giving more autonomy to operating people and allowing work to get done more easily.

The downsizing was accomplished with compassion. Early retirement, with a substantial financial settlement, was the preferred solution throughout the system and, while there can be no question that the process was painful, considerable attention was paid to minimizing the pain in every possible way.

A training program for all BA personnel with direct customer contact—"Putting People First"—was another important part of the unfreezing process. This was the first in a series of different training programs aimed at supporting the change process. It was followed in the movement phase by "Managing People First" and "Leading a Service Business"—programs for executives and managers. These programs were all experiential, and those for executives and managers involved individual feedback to participants about their behavior or management practices on the job.

These training programs all had more or less the same general purpose: to identify the organization's dysfunctional management style and begin the process of developing a management style that would fit BA's new, competitive environment. If the organization was to be market driven, service based, and profit making, it would require an open, participative management style, one that would produce employee commitment.

On the structures and systems level, during the unfreezing stage, extensive use was made of diagonal task forces composed of individuals from different functions and at different levels of responsibility to deal with various aspects of the change process: the need for MIS support, staffing patterns, new uniforms, and so on. A bottom-up, less centralized budgeting process was introduced in sharp contrast to the former one.

The redefinition of BA's business as service rather than transportation was a critical shift on the climate/interpersonal style level. A service business needs an open climate and good interpersonal skills, coupled with outstanding teamwork. Off-site team building meetings were chosen to deal with these issues during the unfreezing stage, processes which now have been institutionalized.

None of these changes would have occurred without the commitment and involvement of top management. Marshall himself initially identified the problem as changing BA's culture and he played a central role in both initiating and supporting the change process, even when problems arose. As one index of this commitment, Marshall made it his practice to attend the Sunday night opening sessions of most training programs—both to "show the flag" and answer questions, as well as provide his unique perspective on what needed to be done.

An important element of the movement phase was the acceptance of the concept of *emotional labor*, the high levels of energy necessary to provide high levels of service in a sometimes uncertain environment such as the airline business. The recognition that such service is emotionally draining and often can lead to burnout and permanent psychological damage is critical to developing systems of emotional support for these service workers.

The retraining of the traditional personnel staff as internal change agents charged with helping and supporting line personnel was an important supportive mechanism. So, too, was the development of peer support groups for managers completing the "Managing People First" training program.

To support this movement, a number of internal structures and systems at BA were changed. Introduction of a new profit sharing program demonstrated the commitment of management to share the financial gains of BA's success. The opening of Terminal 4 at Heathrow Airport provided a more functional work environment for staff. The purchase of Chartridge House as a permanent BA training center enabled an increase and integration of staff training, and the new user-friendly MIS enabled managers to obtain the information necessary to do their jobs in a timely fashion.

The refreezing phase saw the continued involvement and commitment of BA's top management in ensuring that the changes became fixed within the system. Only people who clearly exemplified BA values were promoted, especially at the higher levels of management. New training programs were introduced: "Open Learning" programs including orientation programs for new staff, supervisory training for new supervisors, and so on were augmented by "Top Flight Academies" that included training at the executive, senior management, and management levels, several of which led to MBA degrees.

A new performance appraisal process was created based upon both behavior and performance, emphasizing customer service and subordinate development as key elements. A performance-based compensation system is being installed and the use of task forces continues to solve emerging problems, such as those resulting from the acquisition of British Caledonian Airlines.

Attention was paid to BA's symbols as well—new, upscale uniforms; refurbished aircraft; and a new corporate coat of arms with the motto, "We fly to serve." A unique development has been the creation of teams for consistent cabin-crew staffing, rather than the ad hoc process that is typically used. Finally, there is continued use of data feedback on management practices throughout the system.

Managing Change

The process of change, unfortunately, is not a smooth one, even if one is attentive to Lewin's (1958) model of change. Changing behavior, both individually and organizationally, means inhibiting habitual responses and producing new and different responses that feel awkward and unfamiliar. It is easy to slip back to the familiar and comfortable.

For example, an organization may intend to manage more participatively. But when confronting a difficult decision, it may not be possible to make a consensus decision—at least not initially. The frustration and impatience to get on with a decision can lead to the organization's early abandonment of the new management style.

In moving from a known present state to a desired future state, organizations must recognize that there is an intervening *transition* state (Beckhard & Harris, 1987) that requires careful management, especially when the planned organization change is large and complex. An important part of this change is that management is recognizing and accepting the disorganization and temporarily lowered effectiveness that characterize the transition state. In the BA change effort the chaos and anger occasioned during the transitional phase of the change process now has abated, and clear signs of success have now emerged. But there were many times when the outcome was not at all clear and serious questions were raised about the wisdom of the process both within and without BA. At such times, the commitment and courage of top management are essential.

Managing these organizational changes often may require using a transition management team composed of a broad cross-section of members of the organization to heighten involvement. Other techniques include using multiple interventions rather than just one (Burke, Clark, & Koopman, 1984), keeping the system open to feedback about the change process, and using symbols and rituals to mark significant achievements. The BA program used all of these techniques.

Organization Development (OD)

Like individuals or families, organizations frequently find themselves in need of help, especially when instituting change. Sometimes they need specific content experts—people who can do things that present employees either cannot do or do not have the time to do, such as design a cafeteria-style benefits program or conduct a market research study. (Such experts are readily available, as a perusal of your local Yellow Pages under "Consultants" will quickly reveal.) Often, however, the organization's problems are not so quickly sorted out. The organization can identify certain dysfunctional behaviors, such as conflict; absenteeism; low productivity; and, particularly, all sorts of difficulties in managing the change process. Here the need is to look beyond the symptoms of organizational distress and seek the root cause in the traditional clinical diagnostic model. The BA change effort involved extensive use of this type of consultation.

Organization development (OD) was initially a special kind of organizational consultation process (Burke, 1982, 1987) aimed at uncovering such root causes and generally facilitating organizational change. In the organizational assessment and diagnostic phase of the OD process, OD consultants typically collect data using interviews and questionnaires as well as direct observations and then provide the client organization with feedback on its throughput processes (especially about its internal human interactions) based on those data. Finally, in the intervention phase OD consultants use training, structural changes, role negotiations, team building (Dyer, 1987), and process consultation (Schein, 1969) to facilitate change.

Process consultation—the unique OD intervention—involves the consultant's examining the pattern of communications in an organization. This is done most often through direct observation of staff meetings and, at opportune times, raising questions or making observations about what has been transpiring. The role of the process consultant is to be counternormative—that is, to ask why others never seem to respond to Ruth's questions, or why no one ever challenges Fred's remarks when he is clearly off target. Generally speaking, process consultation identifies the true quality of the emperor's new clothes, even when everybody pretends that they are quite elegant.

Argyris (1970) specified three criteria for OD consultants in facilitating organizational change: (1) valid and useful information, (2) informed choice, and (3) internal commitment. By the first criterion,

Argyris means that the information the OD consultant has collected and fed back to the client system accurately reflects the feelings, attitudes, and concerns of the organization's members and the changes they seek. The second criterion means that the members of the organization, not the consultant, choose what to do about the data, explore the meaning of the data and its implications, and decide how to proceed. And the third criterion means that there is commitment to that planned course of action by the members of the organization. OD interventions that meet Argyris' criteria comprise a set of actions or interventions based upon the understandings and technologies of social psychology and organizational behavior undertaken to improve organizational effectiveness, especially in the management of change.

OD and management. Although OD started as the application by consultants of theory from psychology and organizational behavior, the general management literature and management practices have now adopted many of the concepts, methods, and values inherent in the work of these consultants (Beer & Walton, 1987), a state of affairs that has been greatly aided by the popular writings of Peters and Waterman (1982) and others. Managers now are beginning to talk about their organizations as open systems (Waldbaum, 1987) and acknowledge the importance and nature of leadership and of organizational culture. As noted earlier, it was Marshall who initially identified the need to change the BA culture, not the consultants. Further, managers themselves now design innovative plants, manage participatively, collaborate with unions, use task forces on special projects, and hold off-site team building sessions. This is clearly the situation now at BA. As a result OD consultants, including those at BA, now often find themselves in the role of supporting the changes initiated by managers rather than initiating the changes themselves.

Changing world economic conditions requires a higher level of commitment from employees for organizational success. Hackman (1986) suggested that this pressure for commitment has led at least some organizations and their managers to shift from a top-down management control process to an employee *self-management* process. This process of self-management, according to Hackman's review, leads to significant increases in work unit effectiveness as shown by work unit productivity, problem solving capacity, and work-related contribution to individual growth and personal well-being.

The research evidence. While it would appear that the intervention at BA was a successful one, what do we know generally about the impact of these OD interventions on organizations and their effectiveness? In the past few years, the research literature has shown a sharp improvement in both research design and methodological rigor, especially in the development of hard criteria such as productivity and quality indices (Nicholas, 1982; Nicholas & Katz, 1985). The findings have been surprisingly positive.

For example, Katzell and Guzzo (1983) reviewed over 200 intervention studies and reported that 87% found evidence of significant increases in worker productivity as a result of the intervention. Guzzo, Jette, and Katzell's (1985) meta-analysis of 98 of these same studies revealed increases in productivity averaging almost half a standard deviation, impressive enough "to be visible to the naked eye" (p. 289). Thus it would appear that the success of the BA intervention process was not a single occurrence, but one in a series of successful changes based upon OD interventions.

The picture with respect to employee satisfaction, however, is not so clear. A different meta-analysis by Macy, Izumi, Hurts, and Norton (1986) of the effects of OD interventions on both performance measures and employee work satisfaction found positive effects on performance but *negative* effects on attitudes, perhaps because of the pressure experienced from the new work group norms about productivity. The positive effects on performance, however, are in keeping with the bulk of prior research. A recent comprehensive review of the entire field of OD (Sashkin & Burke, 1987) concluded, "There is little doubt that, when applied properly, OD has substantial positive effects in terms of performance measures" (p. 215). Thus it would appear that OD, which began as a values-based effort to improve the workplace and to develop more effective organizations, may be more effective with the latter than the former—a matter of concern to some OD practitioners, especially those primarily concerned with the compassionate rather than the competitive.

Organizational Culture

The enormous growth of interest over the past few years in organizational culture on the part of both line managers and organizational theorists is a heartening sign of the growing acceptance of social psychological approaches to understanding (and changing) the workplace. The best-selling *In Search of Excellence* (Peters & Waterman,

1982) has provided a new and widely accepted way of understanding, managing, leading, and changing the culture of organizations, despite its limitations as a research study (Carroll, 1983). The interest of BA's Marshall in changing the BA culture reflects the general interest in organizational cultures by senior managers.

Definitional Issues

If we are to understand this subject fully, however, there are two kinds of definitions of organizational culture that need to be identified and clarified. The first defines an organization's culture in terms of what is directly observable—the pattern of behaviors and artifacts prevalent in the organization, or "the way we do things around here" (Deal & Kennedy, 1982). The second is the ideational or embedded definition that defines an organization's culture in terms of the basic assumptions and beliefs widely held by its members regarding human nature, the nature of the world, and so on (Schein, 1985). According to Schein, these assumptions manifest themselves as values on the observable level—values about the way things "ought to be." These values in turn lead to behavioral patterns and artifacts that may or may not be interpretable. Regardless of which definition we use, the observable behaviors must be interpreted if they are to be understood and ordinarily do require speculation about basic, underlying assumptions and beliefs. These speculations can be risky, and the future of *culture* as a useful organizational concept is yet unclear.

To illustrate how such basic assumptions can affect organizational culture, let us consider the basic assumption about the natural competitiveness of human nature. An assumption that competition is inherent in human nature will produce values about the positive consequences of direct confrontation ("We don't pull our punches around here") and the negative consequences of cooperation ("Nice guys come in last"). Such values, in turn, will lead to a combative interpersonal style, a macho corporate image, and a self-protective posture. Sathe (1983) developed a helpful manager's guide to understanding and managing the corporate culture; Schall (1983) applied a communications-rule strategy for analyzing organizational culture; and Martin, Feldman, Hatch, and Sitkin (1983) have provided a schema for script and content analysis of the stories organizations tell about themselves. The use of such structured processes can go a long way to reduce the inherent unreliability of speculations about basic assumptions.

Beyer and Trice (1987) developed a useful typology for understanding an organization through its rites. They identify six major types
of rites:

1. *passage*, to facilitate people in transition into new roles, such as going
   through "boot camp;"
2. *degradation*, to dissolve social identities and their power, such as "drum-
   ming out" a disgraced military officer;
3. *enhancement*, to heighten the status of social identities and their power,
   such as university commencement ceremonies;
4. *renewal*, to refurbish social structures and improve their functioning, such
   as off-site management meetings;
5. *conflict reduction*, to manage conflict and aggression, such as collective
   bargaining to manage union-management differences; and
6. *integration*, to increase bonding among organizational members and commit them to the system, such as the annual office picnic or Christmas party.

These six widespread rites in organizations have both intended and
accidental consequences, and provide a convenient access point for
understanding and managing organizational cultures. The BA change
effort used a number of these rites as part of the change process,
including rites of passage (the new orientation programs are one example), enhancement (for instance, the honoring of people completing the
various training programs), renewal (off-site team meetings), conflict
resolution (direct meeting with union officials to gain collaboration
about particular changes), and integration (a variety of integrative
social functions and parties). In this case these new rites helped cement
or insitutionalize the changes that had occurred.

Variations in Cultures

The strength of organizational cultures refers to how strongly the
members of an organization hold certain basic assumptions. The change-
ability of an organization's culture appears to be a function of its
strength, and this needs to be assessed prior to mounting any change
effort (Wilkins & Ouchi, 1983). Furthermore, large, complex organizations frequently have several subcultures, even if there is a dominant
overall culture. Marketing, production, and research and development
(R&D) are likely to differ from each other and from finance and
corporate headquarters. R&D and finance units may both hold the

dominant organization's basic assumptions about some subjects, but R&D will value innovation whereas finance will value "doing it by the numbers." Martin and Siehl (1983) provide a fascinating analysis of several of the subcultures, including a counterculture, that exist in an organization with a dominant overall culture, like General Motors.

Organizational cultures differ in function over the life cycle of the organization (Schein, 1985). For a young organization, the culture is something to be nurtured, especially if it can be made into a competitive advantage. Schein (1983) provided an interesting analysis of the role of the entrepreneurial founder in creating an organization's culture. In a mature organization, culture can be a barrier to change and innovation; and for a declining organization, the culture may prevent a humane demise. The change strategies for each of these stages will differ. For instance, to change a mature organization that needs to innovate in order to survive in a more competitive environment, multiple leverage points for change are required. Clearly the BA change effort occurred within a mature organization. Once the environment did become more competitive, multiple leverage points were required and used to facilitate change.

Each organizational culture also must be regarded as a subculture of the industry in which it operates and of the total national culture. Recently much has been made of the need for American industry to adopt Japanese management practices. However, Marsland and Beer (1983) pointed out that Japan's superior performance results from the match between its management concepts and its traditional culture. They recommended instead that American management adopt practices that match our societal culture, which is more open and egalitarian, less hierarchical, and more consultative. Thus as noted above, Quality Circles—if they are to succeed—need to take into account the greater individualism, lesser commitment to consensus building, and changed role of first-line supervisors in American companies.

National cultures differ in their basic assumptions about the role of work itself in human life, and naturally these assumptions influence the workplace. All cultures recognize, at least implicitly, that a balance needs to be struck between work and nonwork life in terms of time, energy, and commitment. This balance is dramatically different in the three societies in which I have work experience—Japan, Great Britain, and the United States. The balance in Japan is very much in favor of work, especially for men of the managerial class. They leave the house early in the morning, often six days a week, usually returning late in the evening after their families have had dinner. For Japanese men the dominant reference group is the company and the family is a distant second (Marsland & Beer, 1983). In Great Britain, the balance is different, with the family typically winning by a narrow margin. Having tea breaks, being home in time for dinner, taking holidays with the family, and not allowing work to intrude into family life are characteristic of the British, even of managers and executives, factors that influenced the scheduling of the various BA training events and programs. And the United States is somewhere in between, as our norms vary depending upon the industry and geographical location. There are important lessons here both for adopting the management practices of other cultures and for exporting our own practices.

Culture and Climate

In this context, differentiating organizational culture from organizational climate is worthwhile. As we have seen, culture is a deep construct, always involving an attempt to understand what lies below the observable pattern of behaviors. Climate, on the other hand, refers to the more transient interpersonal or social "weather." Climate encompasses both the formal policies and informal norms that characterize peer and subordinate-superior relationships in an organization and how these relationships are experienced by organizational members; that is, how these relationships make them feel about the organization. Measuring climate typically involves asking organizational members to evaluate their work group along such dimensions as openness, trust, and respect. Climate is most often subsumed as an element of culture, although it has been used as a synonym for culture as well. I find it useful to differentiate the two concepts.

The concept of organizational culture should prove to be a useful, as well as popular, one for organizational change agents as they attempt to understand and change the social psychology of the workplace. Its centrality to the BA situation should be abundantly clear at this juncture.

Cross-Cultural Issues

Organizations often grow through mergers and acquisitions. Considerable attention to the financial strength, market position, management capability, and other tangible aspects of the other organization is always part of the merger or acquisition process. Rarely is any attention given to the culture of the other organization and how it will match that of the acquirer or merger partner. Yet a cultural mismatch is probably even a greater risk than that posed by any of the tangible factors. Given the differences among the cultures of various organizations, what happens when two organizations merge, or one acquires another and there is such a cultural mismatch? Lefko (1987) averred that more than half of these mergers and acquisitions fail primarily because of the clash between the two discrepant cultures and the inability of the management group to manage differences between the two.

For example, the acquisition of the Fireman's Fund Insurance Company by American Express failed largely on this basis. American Express, a financial service company, acquired Fireman's Fund, an old-line casualty liability company, in order to fill a gap in its product line. But American Express did not take into account that its aggressive, high-growth, short-term focus was incongruent with the traditionally conservative, long-term focus of the casualty insurance industry generally and Fireman's Fund in particular. Despite its best efforts to integrate the Fireman's Fund into its operation, American Express divested itself of the newly obtained firm within a year after the acquisition.

As organizations look to mergers and acquisitions as a way of operating more efficiently and profitably in a highly competitive marketplace, they will need to become increasingly sensitive to the issues of differences in organizational cultures and how to manage them. The BA acquisition of British Caledonia recently became a new venue for the application of the concept of organizational culture. British Caledonian was a younger, less structured, and more competitive organization. The consequences of the acquisition needed to be carefully managed in order not to disrupt the still-tenuous changes that had occurred in BA. Again cross-organization task forces, which liberally used process consultation, dealt with many of the emerging issues of the merger.

In another example, the recent merger of two major computer companies—Burroughs and Sperry—organizational psychologists played a prominent role in creating and facilitating transition task forces for various organizational functions, such as accounting and marketing. These task forces were constituted of representatives from each function within both Burroughs and Sperry. Each task force developed a new organizational structure for its function and also worked to reduce the ambiguity and uncertainty that typically demoralize organizations during a merger (Uttal, 1986). The large-scale involvement of a broad cross-section of the two formerly separate and distinct organizations was intended in both cases to increase understanding of and commitment to the merger. The early reports from both of these mergers suggest success, although time will provide richer and more complete data in both cases.

There is also a growing tendency among business organizations, both American and foreign, to develop internationally through the establishment of foreign subsidiaries. When organizations expand overseas, similar cross-cultural problems can arise. As noted earlier, an organization's culture partially reflects the national culture in which it exists. Hall (1977) reviewed the literature in this area and concluded that "the culture of the system surrounding an organization has a major impact on the way the organization operates" (p. 310). Cross-cultural understanding is a necessity for organizations that operate transnationally.

Fortunately, there seems to be more awareness of the role of cross-cultural differences across national boundaries than within them, perhaps because of the clear language differences between many countries. Even so, in a survey of 105 American companies operating abroad, only one third had any sort of formal training programs to prepare individuals for overseas work (Wexley, 1984). On the individual level, such training must go beyond language skills to include a clear awareness of how each of us (and each of our organizations) is culturally bound. On the organizational level, there are great difficulties in exporting management practices from one country to another that need to be modified to fit the new soil into which they are to be implanted.

Torrence (1984) documented the issues involved in translating the Japanese concepts of lifetime employment and wages based upon seniority to a new Kawasaki Motors plant operation in Nebraska. These concepts, which are functional in highly disciplined and culturally homogeneous Japan, simply were not directly exportable to nonconforming, heterogeneous American society. In order to avoid unionism, Kawasaki had to modify its management policies to include an equitable wage and salary system based on both seniority and merit. The company also had to increase job security through cross-training and community relations activities and establish a communications system that was more open than is typical in Japanese industrial units. Any such movement by an organization across national boundaries must consider the impact of the culture of the host country on the move, plan accordingly, and continue to monitor carefully what happens to the organization when crossing cultural boundaries.

Conclusion

I very much believe that the social psychology of the workplace provides all of us—managers, rank-and-file employees and psychologists—with an important and different perspective for understanding and coping with an ever increasingly competitive environment. My purpose in writing this chapter is to share some of this perspective from an admittedly biased point of view. My perspective has been developed from more than 20 years of experience as an organizational consultant and an extensive reading of the relevant literature.

The change effort at BA provides a recent example of how this perspective and understanding has been applied. What should be apparent from this abbreviated overview of a massive project is that the change process at BA was based upon open-systems thinking. Both the design and implementation of this change effort relied on an understanding of the social psychology of the workplace in general and the BA workplace in particular. This was a multifaceted effort that used many leverage points to initiate and support the changes. The change process was intentionally managed with strong support from top management using transition teams with openness to feedback. There was an active management of the resistance to change, using unfreezing strategies at all three levels—individual, structural and systems, and interpersonal. Virtually all the issues involved in organizational change discussed in this chapter emerged in some measure during the course of the project. Energy and space preclude covering these in any further detail, and the work continues.

I have found that consulting with organizations on their planned change activities involves an integration of virtually all of the skills and knowledge of applied psychology—a process that is a continual "stretch" for me and for most of those colleagues with whom I have discussed these matters. Amongst all of us there is a strong feeling that we were developing both the technology and the theory as we worked. It is quite reassuring now to begin to find empirical support for these efforts in field studies and case reports. I am delighted especially that the recent meta-analyses of much of this work are so supportive of what we do. We need to use such reports to help more managers understand the worth of applying the social psychology of the workplace to their change efforts. But we need to remember that only when proof of the usefulness of an intervention strategy is found in their bottom line will most line managers be persuaded that social psychology and the "real world" are not necessarily incompatible. The BA success story is a very useful one for beginning that dialogue.

While there are many difficulties and frustrations in attempting to apply social psychology to the workplace, these are offset by the delicious excitement of being involved in working with managers on issues that affect the lives and careers of large numbers of people and the success or failure of business enterprises, and of actively participating in efforts to make the workplace a better place to be. For me that is a trade-off well worth making!

References

Argyris, C. (1970). *Intervention theory and method.* Reading, MA: Addison-Wesley.

Beckhard, R. (1969). *Organization development: Strategies and models.* Reading, MA: Addison-Wesley.

Beckhard, R., & Harris, R. T. (1987). *Organization transitions: Managing complex change* (2nd ed.). Reading, MA: Addison-Wesley.

Beer, M., & Walton, A. E. (1987). Organization change and development. *Annual Review of Psychology, 38,* 339-367.

Beyer, J. M., & Trice, H. M. (1987). How an organization's rites reveal its culture. *Organizational Dynamics, 16*(4), 5-24.

Bramel, D., & Friend, R. (1981). Hawthorne, the myth of the docile worker, and class bias in psychology. *American Psychologist, 36,* 867-878.

Burke, W. W. (1982). *Organization development: Principles and practices.* Boston, MA: Little, Brown.

Burke, W. W. (1987). *Organization development: A normative view.* Reading, MA: Addison-Wesley.

Burke, W. W., Clark, L. P., & Koopman, C. (1984). Improving your OD project's chances of success. *Training and Development Journal, 38*(8), 62-68.

Carroll, D. T. (1983). A disappointing search for excellence. *Harvard Business Review, 61*(6), 78-88.

Coch, L., & French, J. R. P., Jr. (1948). Overcoming resistance to change. *Human Relations 1,* 512-532.

Deal, T. E., & Kennedy, A. K. (1982). *Corporate cultures: The rites and rituals of corporate life.* Reading, MA: Addison-Wesley.

Dyer, W. G. (1987). *Team building: Issues and alternatives* (2nd ed.). Reading, MA: Addison-Wesley.

Guzzo, R. A., Jette, R. D., & Katzell, R. A. (1985). The effects of psychologically based intervention programs on worker productivity: A meta-analysis. *Personnel Psychology, 38,* 275-291.

Hackman, J. R. (1986). The psychology of self-management in organizations. In M. S. Pallak & R. O. Perloff (Eds.), *Psychology and work: Productivity, change, and employment* (pp. 85-136). Washington, DC: American Psychological Association.

Hall, R. H. (1977). *Organizations: Structure and process* (2nd ed.). Englewood Cliffs, NJ: Prentice-Hall

Katz, D. (1986). The social psychological approach to the study of organizations. *International Review of Applied Psychology, 35,* 17-37.

Katz, D., & Kahn, R. L. (1978). *Social psychology of organizations* (2nd ed.). New York: John Wiley.

Katzell, R. A., & Guzzo, R. A. (1983). Psychological approaches to productivity improvement. *American Psychologist, 38,* 468-472.

Lefko, M. (1987, July 20). Why so many mergers fail. *Fortune,* 113-114.

Lewin, K. (1958). Group decisions and social change. In E. E. Maccoby, T. M. Newcomb, & E. L. Hartley (Eds.), *Readings in social psychology* (pp. 97-211). New York: Holt, Rinehart & Winston.

Macy, B. A., Izumi, H., Hurts, C. C. M., & Norton, L. W. (1986, October). *Meta-analysis of United States empirical change and work innovation field experiments.* Paper presented at the meeting of the Academy of Management, Chicago.

March, J. G., & Simon, H. A. (1958). *Organizations.* New York: John Wiley.

Marsland, S., & Beer, M. (1983). The evolution of Japanese management: Lessons for U.S. managers. *Organizational Dynamics, 11*(3), 49-67.

Martin, J., Feldman, M. S., Hatch, M. J., & Sitkin, S. B. (1983). The uniqueness paradox in organizational stories. *Administrative Science Quarterly, 28,* 438-453.

Martin, J., & Siehl, S. (1983). Organization culture and counter-culture: An uneasy symbiosis. *Organizational Dynamics, 11*(3), 52-64.

Meyer, J. W., & Rowan, B. (1977). Institutional organization: Formal structure as myth and ceremony. *American Journal of Sociology, 83,* 340-363.

Moch, M. K. (1980). Job involvement, internal motivation, and employee integration into networks of work relationships. *Organizational Behavior and Human Performance, 25,* 15-31.

Nicholas, J. M. (1982). The comparative impact of organization development interventions on hard criteria measures. *Academy of Management Review, 9,* 531-543.

Nicholas, J. M., & Katz, M. (1985). Research methods and reporting practices in organization development. *Academy of Management Review, 10,* 737-749.

Olsen, K. H. (1987, July 19). Learning the dangers of success: The education of an entrepreneur. *The New York Times,* p. F2.

Peters, T. (1988). Restoring American competitiveness: Looking for new models of organizations. *Academy of Management Executive, 2,* 103-109.

Peters, T., and Waterman, R. H., Jr. (1982). *In search of excellence: Lessons from America's best-run companies.* New York: Harper & Row.

Porter, L. W., Lawler, E. E., III, & Hackman, J. R. (1975). *Behavior in organizations.* New York: McGraw-Hill.

Ransom, S., Hinings, B., & Greenwood, R. (1980). The structuring of organizational structures. *Administrative Science Quarterly, 25,* 1-17.

Roethlisberger, F. J., & Dickson, W. J. (1939). *Management and the worker.* Cambridge, MA: Harvard University Press.

Sashkin, M., & Burke, W. W. (1987). Organization development in the 1980s. *Journal of Management, 13,* 205-229.

Sathe, V. (1983). Some action implications of the corporate culture: A manager's guide to action. *Organizational Dynamics, 12*(2), 4-23.

Schall, M. S. (1983). A communications-rule approach to organizational culture. *Administrative Science Quarterly, 28*, 557-581.

Schein, E. G. (1969). *Process consultation: Its role in organizational development.* Reading, MA: Addison Wesley.

Schein, E. H. (1983). The role of the founder in creating an organizational culture. *Organizational Dynamics, 12*(1), 13-28.

Schein, E. H. (1985). *Organizational culture and leadership.* San Francisco: Jossey-Bass.

Torrence, W. D. (1984). Blending East and West: With difficulties along the way. *Organizational Dynamics, 13*(2), 23-34.

Uttal, B. (1986, Nov. 24). A surprisingly sexy computer marriage. *Fortune,* pp. 46-52.

Waldbaum, P. (1987, July 24). Motivate or alienate? Firms hire gurus to change their "cultures." *The Wall Street Journal,* p. 19.

Weber, M. (1947). *The theory of social and economic organization* (A. M. Henderson & T. Parsons, Trans.). New York: Oxford University Press. (Original work published 1924)

Wexley, K. N. (1984). Personnel training. *Annual Review of Psychology. 35,* 519-551.

Wilkins, A. T., & Ouchi, W. G. (1983). Efficient cultures: Exploring the relationship between culture and organizational performance. *Administrative Science Quarterly, 28,* 468-481.

PART V

Summary and Conclusions

10 Emerging Managerial Themes for the 1990s: Interdependencies and Synergies Among Individual, Organizational and Societal Well-Being

DANIEL B. FISHMAN
CARY CHERNISS

This book began with the question, How do we reconcile individual employee needs with organizational imperatives in the workplace today? In other words, how can contemporary companies meet increasing competition in the marketplace and still be sensitive and responsive to their employees as people—as individuals with personal aspirations, family responsibilities, and susceptibility to stress reactions with consequent medical and emotional problems?

In Chapter 1, Radigan set the scene for approaching these questions by reviewing important aspects of the business world today: an increasingly global marketplace; changes in the size, gender, ethnic status, and age of the work force; deregulation; the shift from a labor-intensive to a knowledge-intensive, high technology workplace; the shift from a product-dominated to a more service-oriented economy; and the growth of corporate restructuring and takeovers. These forces have contributed to increases in employee disability, as reflected by a workers' compensation claim level in 1987 of $35 billion, double that of 1980. This increase partly reflects an enlarging of the definition of compensable disability to include mental stress on the job and emotional trauma from being fired.

Chapters 2 through 9 then addressed the core questions in a structured manner. The plan for the overall approach is described in Chapter 2 and summarized in Figure 2.1, which is a flow chart of the societal, organizational, and individual forces associated with the new competitiveness conditions in today's marketplace. In this final chapter, we will take two complementary approaches for reviewing the ideas and insights in Chapters 2 through 9. First, we will recapitulate the chapter interconnections in terms of the summary in Figure 2.1. Then, with the summary as a context, we will explore two broad, cross-cutting themes that emerge from the chapters as a whole.

The first theme is the growing interdependencies among various segments and constituencies associated with the business world, including interdependencies between business and education; between companies and the personal lives and families of their workers; between business and government; and among the various stakeholders in a company—executives, managers, supervisors, line staff, and customers.

The second cross-cutting theme is the growing complementarity, or *synergy*, across three segments of American society: (1) the emerging attitudes and values of workers, which are summarized in Maccoby's concept of the self-developer; (2) the requirements of organizations if they are to continue to compete in the global marketplace, which are summarized in Lawler's concept of the high involvement organization; and (3) the American governmental ideal of political democracy.

Recapitulation of Parts II through IV

As outlined in the flow chart in Figure 2.1, the main body of the book, Chapters 3 through 9, is divided into three major sections, Parts II through IV. Part II examines historical, social, and technological perspectives on the the new realities of work and workers. In Chapter 3, Maccoby analyzes forces for increased organizational competition. He argues that to a significant degree, these pressures come from the changing nature of the products and services created by business. More and more these involve a high degree of information technology, which allows them to be tailored to particular, market-driven customer needs. Maccoby coins the term *technoservice* to identify the type of organization competency needed to create these new products and services. In contrast to the traditional paradigm of industrial bureaucracy, technoservice involves such characteristics as "[an emphasis on] networks and teams; flexible work roles with authority based on competence and knowledge . . . and leadership that develops and motivating corporate culture which supports teamwork" (Chapter 3, p. 42-43).

Maccoby views industrial bureaucracy and technoservice in the context of an organizational map in which the east-west direction represents the nature of the product, from standardized to customized; and the north-south direction reflects the type of productivity process, from electromechanical technology to electronic, computerized systems. In this map, industrial bureaucracy and technoservice are end points on a continuum which ranges from the southwest to the northeast corners, respectively.

In Chapter 3, Maccoby also discusses new attitudes and motivations in workers. Traditionally, corporate executives have identified with the role of the expert, who values measurable achievement on the job and autonomy for self and control over others. However, there is a growing trend today for younger professionals, who will be the corporate leaders of tomorrow, to identify with the role of the self-developer, who values a balance among work, family life, and recreation, and who seeks continual learning to insure marketability and for development as a whole person. In addition, a significant number of today's professionals identify with the role of the helper, who values good relationships on the job.

Maccoby concludes by pointing out that self-developers and helpers are potentially better suited to the technoservice world than are experts. For example, the focus on good relationships of the helpers and the valuing of collaborative problem solving by the self-developers are both important aspects of the technoservice culture.

In Chapter 4, Sarason elaborates upon the dynamics of the self-developer. He documents the breakdown, since World War II, of the traditional separation among the work, personal-family, and educational domains of life. Before World War II, the powerful management positions in the workplace were dominated by middle-aged, "straight" white males. Women stayed at home, and minorities typically were assigned to lower-level positions. In recent years, the women's movement, the civil rights movement, and gay liberation have broken down these old patterns and stimulated people to think about themselves, their work, and their careers in new ways which are more integrated with the rest of their lives.

The growing interweaving of working, personal, and social lives is resulting in new interdependencies between private business and public education. These include a new synergy in locating some public education programs in business work sites and in recognizing that if businesses don't help schools to educate the young, those businesses will have to do the job when that generation enters the work force.

Part III of the book considers two reactions to the new competitive forces and work attitudes reviewed in Part II. One reaction, which is addressed by Lawler in Chapter 5, is to utilize human resources in a new and more effective way by creating new cultures and structures in organizations. He describes three ways in which this restructuring of human resources can be done. Strategy I involves doing the old better by introducing innovative procedures in an organization that retains its traditional top-down management model. Strategy II emphasizes the repositioning of corporate assets by forming alliances and networks around the work, wherever a particular task can be completed in the most cost-effective manner. Finally, Strategy III, which Lawler calls high involvement management, is very similar to Maccoby's model of technoservice. In Strategy III, information, knowledge, rewards, and power are pushed to the lowest level in the organization to enhance worker motivation and flexibility for adapting to the knowledge-intensive jobs demanded by new technology.

Lawler argues that Strategy III has the most potential for addressing America's competitiveness problems. Strategy I may include trying to put new programs, such as Quality Circles, into top-down organizations, but the underlying premises of these programs require participative, nonhierarchical corporate cultures in which to function best. And Strategy II, while it rejects top-down management models, does not keep American jobs at home.

In Chapter 6, Harshbarger considers another reaction to the new competitiveness forces and work attitudes reviewed in Part II. This is the alternative of restructuring financial assets by merger and acquisition. Harshbarger traces the tremendous growth in this approach and documents the devastating psychological effects on those workers caught in the abrupt layoffs and downsizing typically associated with mergers and acquisitions. As strategies for dealing with these effects, Harshbarger makes two suggestions. The first is to build up the resilience of the individual managers by exposing them to competency-building environments in present settings so that if these settings are subjected to a merger or acquisition, those individuals are prepared to cope with job loss and are confident and knowledgeable in seeking new positions. Harshbarger's second strategy is to make the organization itself more resilient to major changes by creating and regularly updating a leadership succession plan for it.

Finally, Part IV presents sample approaches for managing the organizational reactions to competitiveness in such a way as to enhance both business productivity and worker well-being. In Chapter 7, Price illustrates the human and financial costs of typical plant closings in top-down management companies by reviewing the case of the "Larck Corporation." Price goes on to show that plant closing is only one method for accomplishing work force reduction. Other methods, such as natural attrition, early retirement incentives, and involuntary part-time schedules, frequently offer alternatives for accomplishing the same financial goals but in a more humane way. This more humane alternative has positive payoffs for the company; it reduces the threat of lawsuits and leaves a workforce in place which is more motivated and loyal. Price concludes by arguing that retraining is the most future-oriented and preventive strategy for the survival of both the organization and the individual worker in an era of high competitiveness, change, and instability.

In Chapter 8, Galinsky considers business initiatives addressing the linkage between work and family life. One is the recent advocacy by business for increased programs in preschool education, and the other involves developing programs for aiding employees to coordinate their work and family responsibilities. These latter programs fall into five business functions: time policies, such as flexitime; leave policies, such as maternity leave; benefits, such as Cafeteria Benefit Plans; dependent care policies, such as Resource and Referral to aid employees in finding child care or elder care; and wellness programs, such as Employee Assistance Plans.

In considering these "family-friendly" business initiatives, Galinsky analyzes the pitfalls that can potentially undermine them. Throughout, she posits that these initiatives should not be viewed as personnel operating expenses, but rather as costs for investment in human capital. As such, she argues, these initiatives will show positive cost-benefit ratios for an organization and don't have to be justified on the basis of compassion for individuals per se.

Finally, in Chapter 9 Goodstein presents a case study in effective organizational change. From his perspective as an organizational development (OD) consultant for the past five years to British Airways, he describes the transformation of that company from a traditional top-down bureaucracy into a high-involvement technoservice organization. As a larger context to the case study, Goodstein lays out the social psychological concepts behind OD. These include the notions of the business organization as an open social system, in contrast to Weber's traditional concept of the organization as a closed bureaucratic system; the nature of organizational structure; an elaboration of Lewin's model of the organizational change process, in which change is differentiated by the level at which it occurs (individual, structural, or cultural) and the stage in which it occurs (unfreezing, movement or refreezing); and the nature and importance of corporate culture.

The Cross-Cutting Themes
of Interdependency and Synergy

There are two broad, cross-cutting themes which permeate the various chapters of the book, those of interdependency and synergy, and these are reflected in the title of this chapter. We end the book with a summary below of these themes.

Growing Interdependencies

The first theme that emerges from Chapters 1 through 9 are the growing interdependencies among various segments and constituencies associated with the business world. Sarason and Maccoby discuss the interdependency between business and education. Business realizes more and more how dependent it is upon the educational system to produce workers suited to business' needs, especially in a world of increasingly knowledge-intensive jobs. Business is helping in this process by advocating preschool education, which includes day care, so that it is feasible for mothers to take advantage of early education opportunities. Also, business is reaching out to educators who see the advantages of linking public education programs with work sites rather than keeping school settings independent from the rest of the community.

A number of authors discuss the importance of viewing education as a lifelong process. Continuing education is an important component of personal growth, and thus it is a high priority for the self-developer whom Maccoby argues will be the corporate leader of tomorrow. Sarason quotes Abelson (1987) on the vastness of the education and training programs that take place in industry: the dollars spent and numbers of company students trained are comparable to the totals experienced by all the country's four-year colleges and universities. Price underscores the importance of continuing education by pointing out that from the perspective of both the organization and the individual, retraining is the most future-oriented strategy for conserving human resources and preventing obsolescence. He cites Polaroid's fundamental Skills Program as a model in this area. Goodstein cites a number of efforts to upgrade and institutionalize continuing training at British Airways as part of their transformation to a high involvement organization. These efforts included purchasing Chartridge House, a new physical facility for a training center which enabled an increase and integration of staff training; and creating a large number of new training programs, such as the Top Flight Academies for senior managers and the Open Learning programs to orient new staff.

Being a student also emerges as an important competency for managers functioning in technoservice, high involvement organizations. Maccoby points out that in technoservice companies, teamwork involving experts from different areas of knowledge is necessary and so managers and leaders need to be open to learning from the expertise of disciplines other than their own. Lawler describes how, in these companies, knowledge and information are decentralized to the lowest practical organizational levels. This leaves the manager not as an expert with superior knowledge who gives orders, but as a coordinator and motivator who helps to empower his or her subordinates. Harshbarger states it in this way:

> Both a learner and a student be. Most managers define their roles as containing some responsibility for teaching or training subordinates. What many managers fail to conclude are their own responsibility to be students and to learn from their people. . . . Learning can be fun. Teaching can be fun. The most effective work groups and the best managers I have known have discovered this. They mix it up and shift roles from teacher to student and back again: managers and subordinates, together, involved in problem solving and learning. (pp. 118-119)

Another emerging interdependency is between companies and the personal lives and families of their workers. Maccoby points out that the emerging self-developers want a more explicit balance among work, family, recreation, and personal development; and Sarason documents the breakdown that has occurred over the past 45 years in the traditional separation among the work, personal, and family domains of life. Lawler talks about the importance of family-friendly policies in the high involvement organization, and Price documents the devastating effect on family life of poorly planned plant closings and other layoffs. Galinsky analyzes the interdependency between work and family issues in detail and shows how an awareness of this interdependency can impact human resource policies in many different areas, such as job scheduling, leave policies, the customization of benefit packages, dependent care policies, and wellness programs.

The interdependence between business and government is highlighted in Galinsky's chapter, which focuses on national policy in work/family initiatives. Health insurance, child care, maternity leave, notification of plant closings, retraining programs for displaced workers—these are only some of the human resource issues about which there is increasing discussion of how government can work in partnership with business. For example, Galinsky cites recent proposals in Congress to fund expanded preschool education with an Act for Better Child Care Services (ABC) or Smart Start program. In a broader context, although not focused on per se by other authors, there is increasing discussion in the United States about the Federal government developing an explicit industrial policy to compete with other countries that already have such a policy, particularly Japan (Dertouzos, Lester, & Solow, 1989). For example, tax incentives could be used to encourage investors to hold onto stocks over long periods of time to create in this country the kind of "patient capital" readily available in Japan.

Finally, regarding this theme, the authors make clear that interdependency as a mode of thinking is a hallmark of the high involvement, technoservice company. Maccoby points out that in this type of organization, there is a high degree of customization of the product for service to the customer's particular needs, thus necessitating communication and interaction between company and customer. In a similar way, Lawler and Goodstein discuss how interdependent managers are with their subordinates in a high involvement setting. Since knowledge and power have been decentralized, the manager gives up hierarchical control and must depend on teamwork and collaboration in working with subordinates, which means a major emphasis upon open communication between managers and subordinates. Harshbarger discusses the importance of holding managers accountable for people development; each manager "must look at his or her people and, with each of them, plan a program for individual development." Thus managers' performance becomes partly based upon the development of their subordinates, creating a close interdependence between the career goals of managers and those who work under them.

Growing Synergy Among the Interests of the Individual Worker, the Organization, and Society

Synergy is used here to refer to the cooperative, complementary functioning of different forces to create a whole that is greater than the sum of their parts. In Figure 2.1 in Chapter 2, there is an arrow B going from the new attitudes and motivations of workers to Lawler's high-involvement management culture. This arrow reflects the fact that the new type of worker, who is discussed by Maccoby and Sarason and labelled by Maccoby as a self-developer, is particularly suited to high involvement organizations. This is the individual who does not make a strong separation among the various areas of his or her life and who seeks a balance among the work, personal development, family, and recreational spheres. This individual is most satisfied and motivated when working in an environment which emphasizes collaborative problem solving, teamwork, close social relationships, open communication, participatory decision making, and encouragement of creativity and flexibility at all organizational levels. As was pointed out in Chapter 2, one of the organizational changes created in reaction to the new dynamics of organizational competition, Lawler's Strategy III, is moving in similar direction as psychological and social changes in worker attitudes and motivation. In other words, there is reason to believe that a particularly effective way of meeting the demands of increased organizational competitiveness, Lawler's high involvement organization, produces exactly the type of corporate environment that the new type of worker is personally seeking.

In sum, there appears to be a growing synergy between the new type of young professional who is likely to become tomorrow's business leader, and the new type of organization which is particularly well suited to meeting the demands of global competition. Moreover, there appear to be two types of synergy between the interests of the self-developer functioning in the high involvement organization, on the one hand, and the interests of the larger society on the other. First, Lawler presents a compelling case that the high involvement organization shows particular promise for making American business as a whole competitive in the global marketplace. Secondly, the value placed on participatory decision making in the high involvement organization reinforces the American ideal of political democracy.

Across the various chapters of the book there is a consensus upon the important contribution that the high involvement, technoservice approach to management synergistically makes to both corporate competitiveness and employee well-being:

- Radigan argues for the importance of collaborative, trusting relationships with mutual caring between management and its employees. The alternative is destructive to the organization, for it engenders "pervasive cynicism, unpredictable outbursts of ill will, overt lack of cooperation, and destructive acts against the corporation" (p. 18).
- Maccoby and Lawler both spell out the strengths of the high-involvement, technoservice organization.
- Sarason describes the complementarity between the high involvement organization and the contemporary, self-developing way in which people think about their work as intermixed with family and personal life.
- Harshbarger describes the advantages of training managers to focus on the development of their generic professional skills. He suggests that this training be done by supervisors who relate to their subordinates in a high-involvement, collaborative manner. These supervisors are in turn held accountable for the effectiveness of their "people development." Once managers receive this training, suggests Harshbarger, they will be resilient enough to withstand the psychological shock of merger or acquisition layoffs in a particular company, and they will be prepared to seek, find, and adapt to a new job.
- Price describes alternatives to the traditional, traumatic approach to plant closings and downsizing—alternatives which not only are more compassionate for workers, but which are less costly in the long run to companies. His thinking reflects the problem-solving approach encouraged in high involvement managers: using flexibility and creativity to create a wide range of alternatives to solving a downsizing problem, the manager puts together that package of alternatives which is best tailored to the particular situation at hand.
- Galinsky describes a variety of work/family initiatives that help the individual worker to adapt to work and family responsibilities. This enhances performance in two ways: it engenders the employee's motivation by communicating an attitude of respect and support for the individual's outside life, and it improves the employee's ability to function by structurally providing the best mode for the individual to accommodate both work and family obligations.

- Finally, Goodstein provides a vivid example of how an industrial bureaucracy like British Airways can transform itself into a high involvement organization utilizing the conceptual framework and technology of organizational development.

We believe that the statement at the end of Lawler's chapter provides a cogent summary of the synergy theme and serves as a fitting note on which to conclude the book:

The high involvement organization seems to represent an important new way for organizations to operate in the United States. It rests on the optimistic assumption that there is nothing wrong with American work or with the United States as a place to do business, but there is something wrong with the way American organizations have been managed. It is clearly not appropriate for all organizations, work, or individuals, but it may have the effect of making work more satisfying for many individuals and perhaps making it possible for many organizations to operate effectively in the United States. In essence, it can end up retaining in the United States work which might otherwise be sent to other countries. More than any other approach, it takes the democratic participative characteristics of the American society and puts them inside the organization from a management systems perspective. Thus it may represent a way for U.S. organizations to be congruent with societal values and at the same time be competitive internationally. (p. 102)

References

Abelson, L. (1987). Editorial: Continuing education for blue-collar workers. *Science, 238*, p. 875.

Dertouzos, M. L., Lester, R. K., & Solow, R. M. (1989). Regaining the productive edge. Cambridge, MA: The MIT Press.

Author Index

Subject Index

About the Editors

DANIEL B. FISHMAN, Ph.D. (Harvard University) is Professor of Psychology in the Graduate School of Applied and Professional Psychology of Rutgers University. Prior to his Rutgers appointment, he was Associate Director for Administration and Evaluation at a comprehensive community mental health center in metropolitan Denver, Colorado. His more than fifty articles and book chapters, and seventy invited addresses, span interests in organizational behavior management, program evaluation, cost-effectiveness analysis, community mental health, behavior therapy, behavioral medicine, philosophy of science, and professional psychology training. He is past President of the Eastern Evaluation Research Society, past President of the Society for Studying Unity Issues in Psychology, and a former Board member of the Association for Advancement of Behavior Therapy. A former Consulting Editor of the *Journal of Community Psychology* and *Professional Psychology: Research and Practice*, Dr. Fishman's books include *A Cost-Effectiveness Methodology for Community Mental Health Centers*; *Assessment for Decision* (with D. R. Peterson); and *Paradigms in Behavior Therapy: Present and Promise* (with F. Rotgers & C. M. Franks).

CARY CHERNISS, Ph.D. (Yale University) is Associate Professor of Psychology in the Graduate School of Applied and Professional Psychology at Rutgers University. From 1972 to 1980 he was on the psychology faculty of the University of Michigan. In 1980 he founded and became the first Director of the Management and Organizational Development Program at the Illinois Institute for Developmental Disabilities. Since arriving at Rutgers in 1983, he has developed a new specialization in Organizational Behavior, and he is currently Coordinator of that program. Professor Cherniss is the author of two books, *Professional Burnout in Human Service Organizations* and *Staff Burnout*, as well as numerous articles and book chapters on the topics of staff motivation, morale, job stress, organizational change, and organizational culture. A Fellow of the American Psychological Association, he has just completed a large, NIMH-funded study on commitment, stress, and professional careers.

About the Contributors

ELLEN GALINSKY, M.S. (Bank Street College) is co-President of the Families and Work Institute in New York City. A former Senior Research Scientist at the Bank Street College of Education, Ms. Galinsky has conducted research on work and family life for the past ten years. Ms. Galinsky also has written extensively about work's impact on the family. She is now serving as President of the National Association for the Education of Young Children.

LEONARD D. GOODSTEIN, Ph.D. (Columbia University) recently completed a term as Chief Executive Officer of the American Psychological Association, an organization of over 65,000 members. In addition to this administrative experience, Dr. Goodstein has had a long and distinguished career as a teacher, management consultant, and author of numerous articles and books on organizational development and change. He currently is a consultant to several multinational firms.

DWIGHT HARSHBARGER, Ph.D. (University of North Dakota) is Senior Vice President for Human Resources of Reebok International Ltd. Before entering this position he was first a management consultant for Rohrer, Hibler, & Replogle, and then Vice President for Human Resources at Sealy, Inc. Before entering industry, Dr. Harshbarger was a Professor of Psychology at West Virginia University, and later an executive director of a community mental health center. He has published numerous research articles in the areas of organizational behavior management, program evaluation, and community mental health.

EDWARD E. LAWLER III, Ph.D. (University of California at Berkeley) is Professor of Management and Organization and Director, Center for Effective Organizations, at the University of Southern California. Dr. Lawler has worked as a consultant for over 100 organizations and has written numerous articles and books, including *Pay and Organization Development, Organizational Assessment*, and *High Involvement Management*.

MICHAEL MACCOBY, Ph.D. (Harvard University) is Director of the Project on Technology, Work, and Character in Washington, DC, and Director of the Program on Technology, Public Policy, and Human Development at the Kennedy School of Government of Harvard University. Dr. Maccoby is a management consultant and social psychologist-anthropologist who has written a number of influential works on social character and management, including *The Gamesman, The Leader*, and *Why Work*. His management consultation has ranged widely, including labor unions (e.g., the United Auto Workers and the Communication Workers of America), corporate management (e.g., AT&T and Westinghouse Furniture Systems), and government (e.g., the State Department and the ACTION/Peace Corps Agency).

RICHARD H. PRICE, Ph.D. (University of Illinois) is Professor of Psychology and Senior Research Scientist at the Institute for Social Research of the University of Michigan. Dr. Price is an internationally recognized leader in the fields of preventive mental health and community psychology and has written extensively about the links between work and mental health. His books include *Abnormal Behavior in the Human Context, Evaluation and Action in the Social Environment*, and *Prevention in Mental Health*. He has recently completed a major study of the impact of plant closings, focusing on the plight of the older worker.

JOSEPH E. RADIGAN, MA (Fordham University) is Senior Vice President for Human Resources at The Equitable Financial Companies, which is the world's third largest insurance company with 25,000 employees worldwide. Before joining Equitable, Mr. Radigan held human resource leadership positions at Donaldson, Lufkin, & Jenrette, a premier investment banking and brokerage firm; General Electric; and Kennecott Corporation, a large, diversified mining and manufacturing company.

SEYMOUR B. SARASON, Ph.D. (Clark University) is Professor of Psychology at the Institute for Social and Policy Studies of Yale University. Dr. Sarason has consulted with numerous organizations and has authored well over two dozen books in many different fields, including *Work, Aging, and Social Change: Professionals and the One-Life, One-Career Imperative; Schooling in America: Scapegoat and Salvation*; and *The Making of an American Psychologist: An Autobiography.*